From school to YTS

Education and training in England and Wales, 1944–1987

Pat Ainley

Open University Press
Milton Keynes · Philadelphia

In memory of Prof. Alan Little,
who tried to make schools work for everyone's benefit

Open University Press
Open University Educational Enterprises Limited
12 Cofferidge Close
Stony Stratford
Milton Keynes MK11 1BY

and
242 Cherry Street
Philadelphia, PA 19106, USA

First Published 1988

British Library Cataloguing in Publication Data

Ainley, Pat.
From school to YTS: education and training in England and Wales. 1944–1987.— (Innovations in education).
1. England. Vocational education
I. Title II. Series
370.11'3'0942

ISBN 0–335–15847–1
ISBN 0–335–15846–3

Library of Congress Cataloging-in-Publication Data

Ainley, Pat.
From school to YTS : education and training in England and Wales, — 1944–1987 / Pat Ainley.
p. cm. —— (Innovations in education)
Bibliography: p.
1. Education, Secondary — Great Britain — History — 20th century.
2. Vocational education — Great Britain — History — 20th century.
3. Education and state — Great Britain — History — 20th century.
I. Title. II. Series.
LA634.A56 1988 373.42 — dc 19 87–37396
ISBN 0–335–15847–1 ISBN 0–335–15846–3 (pbk.)

Typeset by DMD, Oxford
Printed in Great Britain by Oxford University Press

Contents

Series editor's introduction

The eternal triangle of secondary education has written on its sides: education, training and work. Pat Ainley believes that the relationships between the partners has taken three forms since the Second World War and is about to take a fourth. The three forms began in 1944, 1967 and 1977; tripartite, comprehensive and vocational.

Each period was launched by the prospect of new examinations and curricula which would develop the workers of the future, be they skilled, semi-skilled or unskilled. Each period met difficulties of measuring anything other than narrow academic skills or simple manual skills. Having drifted rudderless they became caught on the rocks of 'what employers want' – in times of boom employers do not worry about qualifications and during slumps employers use academic qualifications to reject the bulk and filter out a residue. Then before long each period was sunk by tidal waves of economic and technological change. The key point is their similarity, their cargo of vocationalism. This history is outrageous in its repeated attempts to separate out young men and women into those of 'gold, bronze and iron'.

Ainley's skill lies in researching these periods in their own terms and unearthing the nuggets which express their approaches so succinctly; in showing the connections and continuities between the periods and in tackling directly the key issues of 'occupational choice', examinations and 'transition to work'. His purpose is to show that the assumptions about skills have always been wrong or at the very least out of date. For what the majority face in the early 1990s and beyond is a broad band of semi-skilled work, low paid, often as contract labour and switching from one job to another. Ainley insists that a new period could begin from 1988 onwards which sets up a countervailing force to this 'fate'. His position is one of development and is deliberately opposed to what Giroux had called the dialogues of domination and of despair.

His approach to the vocational period will hold great interest in itself, especially with regard to YTS. Ainley does not labour familiar arguments but nor is the MSC caricatured as wholly bad in comparison with essentially good earlier periods. The charges of creating cheap labour, massaging national employment figures and creating the illusion of prospects for parents and youths alike have to be answered by each period in turn.

Some of Ainley's views on comprehensives and tertiary colleges may be too sweeping for those who have innovated within them and with good faith. Certainly two books in this series, Bernard Barker's *Rescuing the Comprehensive Experience* and David Terry's *The Tertiary College, Assuring our Future*, contribute their own arguments towards Ainley's fourth period. Such a debate could only be healthy. The rise and fall of the MSC as an innovation means yet again there will be a brief moment in which educators can take the initiative on issues of skills, learning, job prospects and citizenship. After from school to YTS, what next?

Acknowledgements

To Isabel Whitfield, Roy Sargesson, Richard Wareing and Jim Bond of the Goldsmiths' College Computer Centre for their help in the transcription of this manuscript. To Naomi Roth and Colin Fletcher for their help and encouragement in bringing it to print. To Beulah for her patience and to Adam for the welcome distractions that he provided and in the hope that he might benefit from better education and training than that described in this book.

CHAPTER 1

Introduction: The politicization of education

The failure of vocationalism and the 'failure' of education

Despite its repeated electoral endorsement, the years of Conservative government since 1979 have seen the failure not only of an economic policy but also of an education policy. Like monetarism in economics, vocationalism in education was first applied in the last years of Labour government. Yet the successive Conservative administrations made both -isms peculiarly their own. However much the employment register is manipulated, monetarism is now plainly discredited by the demonstrable incapacity of market forces to pull Britain out of deepening recession. Vocationalism soon became the Conservatives' educational equivalent of monetarist economics. While the failures of monetarism have been disguised, the failures of vocationalism have simply been forgotten. Recently there has been a dramatic shift back towards traditional academic schooling. This is a perhaps unforeseen consequence of the Conservative manifesto commitment to increase parental choice of school. This will result in competition for entry to schools guaranteeing passes in the examinations necessary for entry to higher education and secure, professional careers. Yet vocationalism is still widely advanced as the solution to the problems of the majority of the nation's schools and colleges. Indeed the relevance of vocational education to the world of work is continually represented on all sides as the means to economic recovery. The results of such an approach to education are less spectacular than the devastation of industry together with the misery of additional unemployment, which have been the price paid by monetarism for a (temporary) lowering of the inflation rate. But the failures of education policy are more insidious: a report by Her Majesty's Inspectors described a national service in which 'Few involved in providing or providing for education can take much, if any, pride . . . within which three tenths of all the lessons seen were unsatisfactory; one fifth was adversely affected by poor accommodation; a quarter was suffering from shortages of equipment . . . [and] the teachers' perceptions of pupils' potential and needs were inadequate' (DES 1985: 12).

The fact is that state education, particularly state secondary schooling, is, stated simply, in a mess. This is not only apparent to the Inspectorate, but has long figured in public consciousness. The Education Minister, Mr Baker, attempts to hide this fact in a whirl of frenetic action, his self-contradictory activities only worse confounding the existing confusion. His predecessor, Sir Keith Joseph, became symbolic of the true state of affairs. As Paul Johnson wrote, he was 'a tragic, bewildered figure . . . overwhelmed by the magnitude of his problems and his own evident incapacity to surmount them . . . like a general after a catastrophic defeat' (*TES* 11/4/86). Yet this was the man who, Mrs Thatcher testified in her letter answering his resignation, 'more than anyone else was the architect who shaped the policies which led to victory in two elections'. One paradoxical consequence of the failure of these policies as applied by their architect to education has been a general politicization of education at all levels.

Education in Britain today has become political. In the 1987 General Election and in the continuing public debate education has had a greater salience than at any time since Harold Wilson promised grammar schools for all in the 1964 General Election, or since the 1944 Education Act seemed to offer a better future to the children of the people who had won the war. An area of life that was previously taken for granted as part of conventional, everyday reality, accepted by all as something everyone goes through, is being increasingly questioned. This does not mean that the place of education in public life has suddenly become transparent. In fact, confusion on the subject has never been greater and this profusion of views and opinions contributes to the sense of crisis in education. For, in becoming political with a big P, education is once again a football in the electoral game played by the major political parties.

Education is also political with a small p, as a subject of conversation as perennial as the weather. Almost everyone can speak of it from their own experience: they went to school themselves, their children or those of their relatives or friends go to schools, or they meet with youngsters whose worrying behaviour can be attributed to their schooling, or lack of it. So education is a subject upon which everyone may have an opinion, especially as, evidently, it can no longer be left to the experts, the teachers, administrators and politicians, those who claim to know best for other people. Furthermore, talking about education is to talk about society itself, what values it should preserve in the young and what shape it should take in the future. Education is also the public arena in which the state touches most directly and regularly upon the lives of its citizens; the juncture, in classical terms, of state and civil society. More than any other public service therefore the present crisis in education epitomizes what is happening to society as a whole and to the post-war welfare state in particular.

The failure of state education has given it this controversial status. Education has failed to achieve the goals which were set for it by politicians and which it largely accepted for itself. It has not, patently, contributed towards social equality and, linked to that, it has repeatedly failed to meet the demands of a modernized economy. Education and educators at all levels are thus blamed for Britain's social malaise and for the country's relative economic decline. From Leon Brittan's claim that 'Indiscipline in our schools has led to disorder in our streets' (Conservative Party broadcast, October 1983) to Lord Young's tirelessly and tiresomely repeated refrain that pupils leave school 'unprepared for the world of work', this has been a constant theme of government pronouncements since the Great Debate on Education in 1976. In fact, of course, rather than education causing the crisis, it is the crisis of society and of its economy which manifests itself acutely in education, especially at the level of secondary schooling.

In state secondary schools all the accumulated contradictions of Britain's recent social development appear to come to a head. There the lack of opportunities for the majority of youngsters are thrown into their starkest relief by the chronic rise in unemployment and by the semi-casualized labour market that is emerging with the application of new technology to replace old industrial processes. Racial conflict that is a consequence of the racism permeating the entire society is endemic to secondary schools where it is only contained with mounting difficulty. Similarly, the position of young women has not improved in a school system that ostensibly offers equal chances to all. Class differences, which comprehensive schools were supposed to ameliorate, have widened and are becoming more pronounced. The end result of the comprehensive reform is now clearly established as effecting educational selection through formal equality of provision in areas differentiated by class residence. Schools, instead of acting as the unifying social force they were intended to be, have now become one of the main polarizing agents separating those who know from those who do.

Shock, horror, boredom

The condition of state secondary schools deteriorates daily and visibly. Shock-horror stories abound of violence by pupils, while from certain newspaper reports, child prostitution and drug-taking would appear epidemic. And it is a fact that more than £25 million is expended annually on repairing vandalism and arson in schools, while it is estimated that £200 million (or 2.5 per cent of the total spending on education) is wasted every year in terms of resources unused due to truancy by 90,000 pupils 'absent without good cause' on any one particular day, according to Mark Carlisle when Minister of Education in 1981. The government's promise to crackdown on truancy in the White Paper *Better Schools* (HMSO 1985a) had no effect whatever upon this problem, beyond establishing an unfounded connection in the public mind between truancy and crime. (In fact, only 8 per cent of juveniles are arrested for offences whilst truanting.)

Feelings of boredom and frustration are certainly rife among Britain's schoolchildren and this is more than the perennial 'whining schoolboy . . . creeping like snail/ Unwillingly to school'. At an extreme these feelings can lead to behaviour dealt with by the 439 special units or 'sin bins', which the *Daily Mirror* reported had doubled in numbers over recent years (7/7/81). While the Advisory Council for Education stated in the same year that it had evidence to show that between 16,000 and 18,000 pupils were being pacified with drugs for 'hyperactivity', an American hold-all term covering lying, stealing, temper, defiance, disobedience, inability to concentrate, violence and aggression. Within the unexceptional mainstream only 35 per cent of a very large sample answered 'not true at all' to the statement 'I don't like school' (Stedman 1980: 149). Since then things have got worse. Even Sir Keith Joseph could see that the reason most secondary schoolchildren are 'bored silly' is because 'they are taught and examined on a curriculum designed for only 20 per cent of them' (*TES* 6/7/84).

Teaching has lost whatever status it once held as an occupation and has forfeited the public esteem to which as a profession it still aspires. Since, for the large majority of secondary school pupils, whatever they do in school has little or no effect upon their progress once they leave and this perception is obvious to them while they attend and affects their school performance, teachers can no longer hold out to pupils the carrot of 'study-hard-for-good-exam-results-to-get-a-good-job'. Increasing disillusion has resulted on both sides, so that 'teacher truancy', through 'illnesses' and other absences, is also a major problem for the education authorities. Again, this is more than the patience which Dr Johnson noted was tried 'by every man that has ever undertaken to instruct others, to recall vagrant inattention, to stimulate sluggish indifference, and to rectify absurd misapprehension'. More teachers are leaving the profession via early retirement or drop-out to other occupations. In 1985, for instance, nearly 26,000 teachers quit the service, including 2,500 heads and deputies. Over the past ten years, the number of heads leaving prematurely has trebled, the number of deputies doubled and the number of senior teachers leaving gone up by a factor of five. There is a national shortage of teachers and not only in specialist subjects.

The attempt by teachers to regain their lost status in economic terms runs into a contradictory necessity to take 'unprofessional' strike action and the prolonged teachers' dispute only added to the atmosphere of crisis in the schools. Unlike other contemporary strikes and threatened strikes (miners, postal workers, railway guards, printers), the teachers' action was not occasioned by new technology. It was basically an attempt to reassert a professional status that had been lost as education was steadily drained of purpose and persistently blamed for the conditions of which it considers itself a victim; to stop, as the NUT's President said in his speech to the 1986 National Conference, 'the reduction of teachers to hourly-paid workers'. This was before the new Education Secretary, Mr Baker, changed the character of the dispute by imposing his own settlement. The teachers' action then took as its first aim the restoration of the Unions' negotiating rights.

The strike contributed to the continuing run-down of the state schools and made private educational provision look increasingly attractive to parents ambitious for their children's success who can afford the fees. This is the case even in those middle-class localities where parents were previously content with the comprehensive status quo. In working-class districts it has also added to the persuasiveness of arguments for a return to some form of selective education through an ostensibly fair examination for all to have a go at. To many working-class parents, this seems preferable to being indiscriminately dumped in the local comprehensive. Paradoxically, it is schools in such socially deprived areas that attract the teachers most committed to the egalitarian ideals of comprehensive education and its corollary, mixed-ability teaching, for such dedication is necessary to sustain working in them. To the parents of their pupils this idealism can appear at best mistaken and at worst as a conspiracy designed to keep their children in their place. These views are often encouraged by those who purport to act on behalf of 'the bright working-class child' – and who does not consider their own child bright? – whom the comprehensives are alleged to have failed.

Those who struggle to keep faith with the reforming ideals of comprehensive education can claim that without their efforts the situation would indeed be even worse. More pupils now leave school with examination results of some sort than ever before (nearly 90 per cent). More too pass A levels, though ironically, more fail them also, because the numbers taking the examinations are at a record high. Less leave at the earliest opportunity, Easter, without taking exams (only 10 per cent of boys and 8 per cent of girls). And, while the anticipated increase in numbers remaining beyond the statutory school-leaving age due to rising youth unemployment has not taken place – from their 1983 peak of 28.9 per cent of all sixteen-plus pupils they fell to 26.7 per cent in 1985 – numbers in full- and part-time Further Education have risen to nearly two million. Neither has truancy risen as dramatically as is supposed; in fact, the level of attendance seems remarkably constant over time. In London, where the problem is supposed to be worst, 'The percentage attendance achieved in 1906 by the work of the London School Board and the L.C.C. (89% in all Board Schools) has hardly been excelled in later years. Since 1945 attendance figures have been calculated separately for primary and secondary schools. The former varying since 1950 between 85 and 90%, the latter between 85 and 92' (Rubinstein 1969: 114). The figures still hold true, the drop in attendance being only –2 per cent overall from 1976 to 85.9 per cent in 1986; this despite the reported increases in under-age working in the capital as elsewhere and the attempts by the political opponents of the ILEA to beat that authority with the stick of the allegedly exceptionally high absence rates for London schools.

Neither have periodic scares that levels of literacy and numeracy are falling in the state schools much reality in performances recorded by standardized reading tests. Despite the blandishments of the aural and visual pop and video culture to which most young people primarily relate, the research consensus is of a rise in reading standards overall. Attention centres upon 'the small but disturbing numbers of pupils' an Inspectors' report recorded 'who could barely read and write at the end of the fifth year' (HMSO 1979: 78). This is also alleged to be a constant number: 'Few who actually work with children will quarrel with a pragmatic figure for this sector of around 15%. A constant

15%' (Webster 1982: 11). The percentage is not randomly distributed by social class however: 'As you move down the social-economic class scale, kids read and write less and less well' (Martell 1976: 107). Certainly, two million adult illiterates in Britain show that, after over a century of state education, universal literacy has still not been achieved and this experience is replicated in all of the industrially developed countries.

Primary schools are widely accepted by all the parties involved – pupils, parents and teachers – as laying the foundation for functional numeracy and literacy. There disputes may arise over means but not ends. In secondary schools it is the whole purpose of education which is problematic. Research has shown that even in their basic use of reading and writing many secondary pupils mark time or even regress (Galton and Willcocks, summarized in the 1984 Hargreaves Report for the ILEA, para. 3.3.1). But it is the failure to educate in the wider sense of understanding that is particularly galling to those who looked to state education to liberate the mass of the population, and has rendered groundless the nineteenth-century fears of those who opposed any instruction for the working class. Not only has comprehensive education failed to raise standards for all to equal or challenge the mastery of culture and science by an elite, it finds its place in sustaining popular ignorance, instilling in the majority an acceptance of their relative brainlessness and worthlessness. In the words of a sympathetic observer, comprehensive schools have become 'a humane and even relatively enjoyed form of gentling the masses' (Halsey 1972: 11).

Comprehensives have failed to end juvenile delinquency, as Anthony Crosland, one of their political architects, hoped that they would. Rather, the peak age for juvenile delinquency persists in rising to the year before school-leaving age. Lately comprehensive schools have been accused by government of breeding 'a yob generation' (Patten, 4/4/86). They are also, predictably, repeatedly blamed for football hooliganism.

What went wrong

This catalogue of failure and blame seems far removed from the 1960s when educational expenditure rose above national spending on defence for the first and last time. In that era of expansion, enlightened theories of child-centred teaching were applied to primary practice, the comprehensive reform of its secondary level and the gleaming towers of the new colleges and universities seemed to offer both the means of personal advance to new and better opportunities for many and the possibility of national progress for all. The marriage of education and science promised a new industrial revolution in which, with modernized manufacturing, Britain would once again lead the world. What went wrong is a question that is now not only directed at education. As the health service is reduced to a poor shadow of the private hospitals, as high-rise flats are demolished and housing estates deteriorate into new slums, while the state systems of insurance, benefits and pensions degenerate into new mechanisms for manipulating poverty and managing the poor, it is a question posed for that whole period of social democratic reform.

To those who did not live through it but were born after it, or to those memories extend beyond it to the poverty and depression before the war, it is obvious that the long boom of the post-war period was anomalous and unique. It was the mistake of those who lived through it and were born into it to assume that living standards would continue to rise forever and that the mechanisms of economic control had been discovered which could avert any return to the periodic booms and slumps of the past. With what Blackwell and Seabrook call 'the Second Coming of political economy in our time' (1985: 111), the superstructure of social services that had been created during the long period of growth is no longer sustainable. Britain's economic base is insufficiently modernized to withstand the loss of its previously secure and privileged position in world markets plunged into a new slump and assailed by numerous and more aggressive competitors.

Two political solutions have been advanced by the major parliamentary parties to escape seemingly inevitable economic decline and accumulating social disaster. One offers some sort of return to the social democratic tradition of reform and consensual control of the economy through Keynesian or neo-Keynesian means that worked in the recent past. The other, advanced by Mrs Thatcher's authoritarian populism, acknowledged that it was no longer possible to maintain the old consensus in the running of the economy and that the social services that it afforded would have to be severely curtailed in the interests of capital accumulation. The reduced surplus could only afford what has been called 'a residual welfare state'. To achieve such a social and political reversion and create the conditions in which new industries could at last rise from the ashes of the old, required an accompanying cultural counter-revolution. Old values of thrift, self-reliance and initiative had to be revived in place of the extravagant spending, self-indulgence and reliance upon the state that were perceived as having become habitual. This reassertion of the real and abiding virtues that were supposed to have first brought Britain to world preeminence would, it was promised, finally vanquish the country's unique social malaise.

This inherited 'British disease', so often commented upon by foreign observers, has long valued the practice of effete arts above the creation of wealth necessary to maintain them. The replacement of these acquired attitudes and values by those of an enterprise culture implied a central place for education. At all levels the education system was seen as encouraging attachment to attitudes of dependence and egalitarian lassitude in the majority. These attitudes, together with traditional prejudices for an outmoded culture instead of the entrepreneurial skills required of a managerial elite, are posited as the cultural core of the British sickness. Economic renaissance was thus seen as dependent upon a cultural rebirth in which the role of education was central.

The new cultural transformation in changing attitudes to work that was demanded of the education system required more direction from the central state than the previous sharing of powers with local authorities allowed. 'It is the balance of this partnership which the government intends to change', as Chris Patten told *New Society* (11/4/86). This was to be achieved through specific grants from the centre earmarked for particular purposes, as recommended in the January 1986 Green Paper *Paying for Local Government*. Meanwhile local authority domination of governing bodies was ended by the 1987 Education Act. In this sense too education acquired its new, directly political character. The 1976 Great Debate articulated government's concern that education could no longer be left to the educators, but '. . . industry, the trades unions and commerce should now be involved in curriculum planning processes' (HMSO 1977: 33). Since then the tendency towards direct, central control has accelerated. Under the Conservatives it took a new form. Characteristically, established procedures were bypassed. Apparent autonomy and release from bureaucratic control in favour of determination by market forces were combined with an actual increase in centralization and direct control. Before Mr Baker's advocacy of 'parent power' to encourage new, direct-grant schooling, the paradoxical combination of central control and market freedom was largely imposed upon education by the Manpower Services Commission, a branch of the Department of Employment. Where previous efforts to reshape education attempted to implement the desired changes from within the education service itself, the MSC was used to impose changes from without. The logic of this intervention was to bring education at all levels more directly under the unmediated control of the central state.

The seemingly instinctive and irresistible tendency of the state to increase its powers and centralize direction is evident in many different areas of public life and could be said to typify its response to dire economic crisis. It is continuous with a process that took a different, but more direct, form under previous governments, where actual measures for greater centralization and control were usually combined with apparently increased public participation. Under the latest Conservative governments the process of centralization has been obscured by the commitment to 'rolling back the frontiers of the state'. Nevertheless actual state control, of the labour market for instance, increased to the point where over a million people were employed by the state, directly or indirectly, on various MSC programmes. This represented an unprecedented intervention in the supply and control of labour by a government supposedly committed to the market's freedom from state control.

Propaganda, ideology and equal opportunities

It is not just the increase in power of the central state that has politicized education. Despite amendments to the Education Act outlawing political bias in schools, it can be argued that, as a part of the state apparatus, education has always been political. Though not directly ideological in the way education is used in so-called totalitarian societies, this too has been suggested. In 1950 a Conservative Party Political Centre pamphlet 'One Nation' argued that 'So long as the "cold war" against communism continues, education is more than a social service; it is part of defence' (quoted in CCCS 1981: 63). Whilst this attitude survives in the continuing debate over 'peace studies', it was also Sir Keith Joseph's belief that 'Schools should preach the moral virtue of free enterprise and the pursuit of profit' (speech to the Institute of Directors, March 1982). Indeed, the government has long talked of the need for schools to cultivate 'positive attitudes towards work', as the 1985 White Paper *Better Schools* put it. Given the general acceptability of vocationalism, it is not strange that such demands are deemed politically neutral. Politics, it is generally accepted, should be kept out of education and training (see p. 96), especially when the antiracist, antisexist initiatives of elected local education authorities can be branded as 'loony left' propaganda. And yet it can be argued that there exists 'a huge hidden curriculum . . . teaching the majority a sense of their own relative incompetence and impotence' (Halsey 1972: 11). This message is conveyed much more effectively by omission and confusion than by any amount of direct and organized propaganda.

In any case, despite the efforts of teachers committed to 'peace studies', the armed forces have always maintained a presence within schools and not only for recruitment purposes. Lately they have been joined by the police, who now offer a complete 'Programme for Secondary Schools' entitled 'Living in a Law Abiding Society'. Supplemented by talks, films and visits, this divides into prepackaged sections appropriate for different years and set out in a familiar way for teachers. It begins with a set of 'aims and objectives', the last of which is that 'They [pupils] will adopt a responsible attitude in all their dealings with the police'. Baroness Cox, by a further amendment to the 1987 Education Act, compelled school heads to accede to police requests for a presence in schools and even for governors to pay regard to the views of Chiefs of Police when deciding on school curricula.

Such direct intervention aside, the key ideological commitment of state education is to equality of opportunity. This was the goal which was to have been served by the 1944 reform of education and it was upon these grounds that it was criticized for failing to provide the equal chances that it promised. When Wilson followed Gaitskell's earlier letter to *The Times* in presenting comprehensive schools as 'a grammar school education for all' (5/7/58), he particularly appealed in the 1964 election to that section of the middle class that had to be won over from the Tories. So that 'The emotional impetus against the eleven plus came largely from those parents – middle-class or with middle-class ambitions – who feared seeing their children condemned to working-class modern schools' (Hinton 1979: 32).

Equal opportunity proposed through market mechanisms before which everybody is supposedly equal the theoretical possibility of escape from working-class occupations. So that, 'The actual possibility of social mobility for the exception becomes the primary illusion of an entire class' (Levitas 1974: 53). From this perspective 'We can now see social mobility as an ideology' (Sarup 1978: 185). It is an ideology that changed economic circumstances have increasingly called into question. How far it can be sustained in a depressed economy will be vital to the success or failure of the government's efforts to substitute for conventional, academic examinations as the passports to success new, work-relevant assessments. These technological competencies profiled by the MSC on the Youth Training Scheme, for instance, are supposed to lead the majority of school leavers to the nirvana of regular employment.

Already the apprehension of the social mobility ideal has been altered by the change in schools following comprehensive reform. 'To "fail" within the post-war education system with its underlying meritocratic ideology, where all had "equal" chances to succeed, was a radically different experience to failing in the more openly class-based system of the pre-war years. In the former case, onus for failure rested on the individual's "merit" or "ability"; in the latter on one's social position: a position that has made "educational failure" much harder to bear in the post-war period – and the more galling if one's parents, too, believed the myth' (Clarke and Jefferson 1975: 14). There are indications that sections of the community no longer subscribe to that myth: 'The black sections of school pupils have demonstrated through their behaviour that they can no longer look on schools as a way of getting better jobs. They view them as institutions of discipline which take their time and waste it. The Black Parents Movement has followed the pupils' experience and, unlike previous parents' organisations in the black movement, can no longer see school as an instrument of social mobility' (*Race Today* editorial 1/76).

The ideology of equal opportunities can no longer legitimate economic inequalities through the ostensibly objective and meritocratic mechanism the reformed school system provided for assigning individuals to unequal economic occupations. These inequalities are widening with the restructuring of the working population required for industry's survival and with the application of new technology to all levels of production and distribution. 'Opportunities to be unequal', as Mrs Thatcher translates equal opportunities, must therefore be increased by direct government intervention in the school system. This can only saddle government itself with responsibility for resolving the accumulated contradictions within the educational arena. This responsibility could previously be avoided due to the division of powers in educational administration and by government acting indirectly upon local authorities through rate capping and via the MSC. In this way also education has become directly political and subject to the vagaries of electoral fortunes and their increasing fiscal and media manipulation.

The essential contradictions within education over which government is now taking unmediated control are inherently irresolvable in the present economic and social conditions. The slump in demand for labour and deskilling for many remaining jobs pose the same question of purpose as is put to the MSC's training and retraining programmes. Moreover, the insistence upon work-related education conflicts with the ideal of humanist, all-round education espoused by many teachers, who are in any case neither trained nor equipped to deliver the new training packages. Most working-class parents, however, do not subscribe to this middle-class ideal of education for its own sake, which can be seen as an ideology masking the ambition for the security of a career. Instead they are pragmatic in their demands upon schools. They are therefore susceptible to promises of vocational relevance in education. Nor is the demand for vocational education necessarily misguided; as will be suggested in conclusion, a genuine vocational education could harness the mechanical and computational powers of new technology to increase human creativity and intelligence.

The attractions of selective schooling for many working-class parents can be explained in relation to their own experience of comprehensive schooling for their children (and increasingly, by their own direct experience of it as former pupils themselves). However, the proposals for selective state schools floated repeatedly by government cannot be guaranteed to further heighten any more than the existing divisions between middle and working class. For, whatever new divisions within the working class may be opening up as a result of recession, children of employed and unemployed workers are equally likely to pass or fail any new form of selection due to the cultural homogeneity of the class as a whole. Only payment for a different education can possibly guarantee a perpetuation of these material inequalities to new generations, as it already does for those paying for their children to attend private schools. The inclusion of provisions in the 1987 Education Act to allow schools to charge for so-called 'extras', like musical tuition, sports equipment and art materials, moves the state system in this direction (see also p. 140).

The real choice

The real choice before government for education therefore is not between continuing comprehensive education and a return to the traditional values and disciplines of an academic schooling based upon the excellence of the grammar school model. It is between an integrated system of education and training and an immediate release of the state schools to market forces with their consequent more or less rapid privatization. Under Conservative government the former could be but a step on the road to the latter. The MSC has already established the precedent for private managing agents in the Youth Training Scheme and industry is constantly being urged to finance training and parts of education for itself. However, private industry is understandably unwilling to pay for education and training that it does not really need. Further, privatized schooling, through competitive entry to direct-grant schools financially independent of local education authorities, will heighten class differences and antagonisms still more. Direct payment for all education would also radically alter the implicit social contract between the state and citizens to provide services in return for taxes. Such a radical alteration is not inconceivable for a government that has finally abandoned all commitment to the post-war consensual agreement to maintain full employment, that has run down the health service in favour of private medicine and insurance schemes, proposed private instead of state pensions and has sold off 'the family silver' of nationalized industry. In the mixed economy of education that presently exists the Conservatives have sharpened the competitive edge of the private schools by granting them and fee-paying parents further tax privileges and by subsidizing them through the Assisted Places Scheme.

The private schools, and the academic establishments of the antique universities which sustain them through their examination and entrance procedures, have ceased to be the main target – even in rhetoric – of Labour's proposals for further reform of education. Instead there is broad agreement with the suggested integration of education and training. As the *Times Educational Supplement* commented on 'Education and Training' by a Labour Party study group, there is little in the options that they present with which Lord Young would disagree. In fact one of the proposals offered for discussion suggested the same amalgamation of the DoE and the DES with which the Lord of Grafham pressed his own candidacy for Sir Keith's vacancy. Instead of a two-year YTS the study group proposes 'a two year studentship' (renamed 'Foundation Programme' in Labour's 1987 Election proposals). Like the original suggestion for YTS, this would be for all young people, employed and unemployed alike. It is seen as part of 'a comprehensive and integrated tertiary system' to create 'a single system post-16 serving both young people and adults, enabling entry, re-entry, update progression and credit for experience'.

An integration of education and training has long been the goal of the MSC. While it has the same jargon the MSC also has a more radical extension of universally applied profiling and criterion-based assessment than any advocates of new and more practical records of accreditation. Bryan Nicholson, the last Chairman of the Commission, was shrewdly suggested by Jackson as 'The man who could restore the Commission's respectability in good time for the next election and the possible return of a Labour government' (1986: 39). In the event this was not needed; nevertheless Nicholson patched up the rift with local authorities caused by his predecessor Lord Young's insistence that the MSC take over funding of a quarter of all non-advanced further education (as proposed in the 1984 White Paper *Training and Jobs*). Nicholson also took the trouble to give interviews in *New Society* (13/6/85) and in union journals, where he appeared 'On the Side of the Angels' (*The Teacher*, 31/3/86). This was all the more necessary with the return of a Conservative government for a third term when Lord Young departed from overseeing the MSC to bring enterprise to the inner cities. This indicated that the Commission might at last fall into disfavour with the government. Its enjoyment of boundless financial largesse was immediately curtailed with the transfer of Jobcentres to the direct control of the new Minister of Employment and the loss of 15 per cent of the MSC's budget. Whether because he saw which way the wind was blowing, or because of his conciliatory attitudes, or because he opposed the introduction of compulsory YTS and JTS, Nicholson resigned his Chairmanship soon after the 1987 Conservative election victory.

Neither the Labour Party's proposals nor for that matter the SDP's alternative version as presented by Mrs Williams (1985) would alter the division between middle- and working-class youth post-sixteen. This division has been heightened by the virtual collapse of academic sixth forms in working-class areas. Their replacement in Labour-controlled education authorities by tertiary colleges is a rationalization that will probably further reduce the numbers of working-class pupils attempting entrance to higher education. The prevocational skills training that is now offered on equal terms to, and in tertiary colleges in the same building as, the traditional academic perpetuation of an elite, in fact has a quite different pedigree. 'The prevocational model is essentially a variant in the nineteenth century elementary tradition designed to control rather than emancipate the masses' (Whitty 1983: 105). It is risible therefore that Lord Young can assert that a YTS leaving certificate (when, if ever, it appears) will be as valuable as A levels.

It was another irony that the government found itself in conflict with the teachers' unions over the introduction of an examination that the NUT first proposed in 1969. Although designed for only the top 60 per cent in ability, GCSE is intended to unify preparation for two quite different educational outcomes post-sixteen. Although one GCSE paper gives the appearance of equal chances for all, instead of relegating a majority to the second best CSE, those answering the more difficult and extended questions set by the GCE board will be the same top 20 per cent marked off from the remainder by 'merits' and 'distinctions' as effectively as separate O level papers did in the past. Beneath such essentially cosmetic reforms, the shape of the new tripartite structure of secondary schooling becomes clear and is more or less agreed by all parties. Its likely shape in practice is as plainly apparent as it already is in tertiary modern FE where it is well established. Whether the technical stream beneath the top academic 20 per cent attend specially instituted City Technical Colleges, or whether they can be accommodated within an expanded TVEI inside existing schools is really a matter of detail.

The abiding problem for government as it takes more direct control of education is the majority of youngsters in the new secondary modern/comprehensive schools in working-class neighbourhoods. These pupils already present the most acute problems for the day-to-day management of secondary schools, despite the attempted introduction of new methods of assessment designed to manipulate and control them. While they are promised relevance to working life, their schooling is made more irrelevant to the lives they are likely to lead by the removal of any opportunity to use any skills and knowledge that they might have acquired through education. While alternately counselled and cajoled into accepting a 'more adult' responsibility for a situation not of their making, their period of dependence upon the state and their families is being rapidly extended (to as much as twenty-five years in the proposals of the Fowler Review). It has not escaped notice that 'While a few years ago school leavers without qualifications of any kind had no difficulty in getting jobs, many of them are now deemed to need "work experience" before they can be regarded as employable' (Showler and Sinfield 1980: 117). Attempts to force this majority into compulsory YTS by the withdrawal of benefit rights, promised for 1986 in the 1985 Budget, have already occasioned the largest school student strike in British history when a quarter of a million pupils protested up and down the country in April 1985.

This is the 'yob generation' for whose condition government can no longer blame educational administrators and teachers as it assumes direction of education for itself. Neither can it lightly divest itself of the responsibility for them that it has undertaken by cutting loose the secondary schools into the play of the market. Such a refusal of responsibility would put at risk the reproduction of labour power in the future at a time when there are already worries enough about the loss of labour disciplines in the absence of real work and a possible weakening of the work ethic among the long-term unemployed. It also threatens a real crisis of social control in the less 'successful' schools that do not opt out of the state system to which the majority of pupils will perforce be relegated.

The threat to public order which the state is striving to contain is underlined by a racial dimension to the growing class polarization. Like a chemical added to clear liquid to indicate the flow of current, the aggregation of ethnic minority youth in the lower and special streams of secondary schools, in inferior Mode B and Premium Place YTS programmes and subsequently on the unemployment register, has always punctured the pretensions to fair and equal provision of these new arrangements. This has always been apparent to Asian and black parents who have never shared the colour blindness of the official view of equal treatment irrespective of race. Indeed, immigrant communities in general always place great demands upon education. Traditionally they saw schools as ladders of escape from the ghetto for their children and they were never a party to the historical compromise which the indigenous working class made with the status quo. But here again the state is involved in intractable contradictions. Within schools apparently liberal policies of curricular reform have been advanced, while beyond the school gates repression of black people and their communities has increased. This contradiction also affects the local state where elected LEAs have attempted to introduce anti-racist policies for which they gained a mandate from black voters, as in Brent. Further, the long-term material and cultural decline of many working-class areas continues to reproduce a virulently racist ideology, which neither the state nor its schools, nor it seems any independent force, is able or willing to confront with an explanation of its real causes. This could hardly be expected of the state since the integration of this racism and chauvinism has been vital to the construction of Thatcher's populist support. Also the demands of racists within the Conservative ranks remain an option for that party faced with continuing economic stagnation and rejection of its other policies.

Rather than speculate about future possibilities, however, the social realities of the present situation must be grasped to understand the current politicization of education and its likely development and various consequences. To do this the accepted divisions of labour and knowledge between classes in society must be confronted, together with the role that education plays in sustaining them. It must be asked whether the presently agreed approach to education and training will really produce the skills needed for the technology of the twenty-first century. Such an interrogation must go beyond a denunciation of the failure of the latest policy of vocationalism in education. It must look at the failings of the comprehensive schools which this vocational policy was intended to correct and before that to the tripartite system to which comprehensives in their turn were seen as the solution. The common assumptions underlying these three major approaches to education and the economy can thus be clearly revealed. The latest crisis in education is then seen as a part of the economic and social crisis precipitated by recession and insoluble in itself without some resolution of that more general crisis. Only with such an historical understanding can we begin to comprehend what is happening as education becomes political and so begin a new and real Great Debate on Education.

CHAPTER 2

The tripartite system (1944–1964)

Divisions of labour and divisions of knowledge

The 1944 Education Act is the foundation stone of the post-war education system created by the welfare state. As such, it has remained fundamentally unchallenged until Mr Baker's 'great' education reform proposals of 1987. It did not, however, establish a system of equal education with open access to all. Instead, following the recommendations of the 1943 Norwood Report, it introduced what became known as the tripartite system of secondary modern, technical and grammar schools. The Norwood Report had divided the male school population into three inherently unequal groups, for whom three different types of education were appropriate. First, there were those 'interested in learning for its own sake'. These would be able to benefit from higher education and so go on to the management and professional positions in post-war society. Then there were those who, while not so able intellectually, were capable of applying knowledge practically: 'He often has an uncanny insight into the intricacies of mechanism whereas the subtleties of language construction are too delicate for him.' This did not mean that these boys could not talk but they were presumed to be the future skilled workers for the reconstructed economy. Lastly, there were the below-average who were '. . . incapable of a long series of connected steps'. This did not mean that they could not walk, but they were assumed to be the unskilled workers of the future.

Social class was not even hinted at by Norwood as the

criterion for allocation to one of these three grades of being. Indeed, 'Whether such groupings are distinct on strictly psychological grounds, whether they represent kinds of minds, whether the differences are differences in kind or in degree, these are questions which it is not necessary to pursue' (HMSO 1943: 201). In fact, they followed the oldest and most traditional differentation between manual, blue-collar wage workers and non-manual, white-collar, salaried staff. Within this basic distinction between manual and mental labour, wage rates within British industry for hourly paid workers were based upon levels of skill. However inadequately defined, skilled, semi-skilled and unskilled were recognized as categories in the wage structures of most industries and in the class structure of society. Women were not included in this subdivision of the workforce which was defined as male. 'Women's work' was considered separately from the real, bread-winning work upon which the family wage depended. In any case, it was supposed that with the return to normal conditions, women would retire from war production in the factories and farms to the wifely role of reproduction in the home.

On a similar biological basis Norwood echoed the earlier Spens Report in isolating the critical determining factor of 'general intelligence' measurable by intelligence testing. Spens believed that 'intellectual development during childhood appears to progress as if it were governed by a single factor . . . [which] . . . appears to enter into everything which the child attempts to think, to say or do' (quoted in Levitas 1974). Norwood arbitrarily proposed that this socially neutral, genetic endowment was best measured at eleven-plus, when most children transferred from primary to secondary schooling. At this age objective intelligence testing would determine their allocation to one of the three types of school – grammar, technical or secondary modern. This convenient trisection of (male) children into three levels of intelligence – the academic, the technical and the practical – corresponded not only to what were assumed would be the needs of the reconstructed economy, but also to the Ancient distinctions between the men of gold, bronze and iron. The presumption '. . . that the Almighty had created three types of child in just those proportions which would gratify educational administrators' was ridiculed at the time (Curtis 1952: 144–5). Nevertheless such a division has recurred in different forms many times since and it became the long-term goal of the social democratic reform of education to eliminate it in favour of an equal access for all individuals, presumed instead to be innately equal in their abilities.

The immediate target of educational reform at the moment of Labour's establishment of the welfare state remained the long-hated and much excoriated public schools of the upper or ruling class. This 'barbarity' and 'the hereditary curse upon English education', as Labour's foremost advocate of reform had called them (Tawney 1931: 142, 145), was excepted from the provisions of the new tripartite system of schools. Just as the ruling class itself – 'those persons economically free and accustomed to responsibility from an early age', in the splendid phraseology of Sir Ian Fraser (quoted in Marwick 1980: 159) – was somehow absent from accounts of the workforce: as if judges, generals, first-division civil servants and directors of industry were not a part of society and its economy.

The social democratic solution to the continued existence of the public schools lay '. . . in the state providing educational opportunities of such wide variety, encouraging experiments so comprehensive in character, and planning and staffing its schools to provide such high standards of teaching and amenities that no parent, however rich or however snobbish, could gain any advantage either in prestige or social opportunity by paying £315 per year to maintain his son at Eton' (quoted in Green 1948: 161). As 'Red' Ellen Wilkinson, the first Labour Minister of Education, put it to the 1946 Party Conference: 'Free milk will be provided in Hoxton and Shoreditch, Eton and Harrow. What more social equality could you have than that?' (quoted in Vernon 1982: 214).

However, over time, as the hereditary and financial advantages of these schools continued to exert such an unfair influence in the competition between state and private sectors, they came to be the target – at least in rhetoric – of further promised reform. Even today Labour is still committed to abolishing the independent schools, though it is now envisioned that this process will consume the life of more than one Parliament. The Alliance too say they intend to close the widening gap between the state and private schools, while maintaining the 'Right to educational choice' for those able to pay for it. Ironically though, as Halsey noted (1980: 220), it is the Conservatives, with their scheme of assisted places to these schools, who have blurred the distinction between state and private education in a reinvented hybrid direct-grant system.

Also in 1944, in the White Paper *Employment Policy*, the government for the first time accepted 'as one of their primary aims and responsibilities the maintenance of a high and stable level of employment' (Cmnd. 6527). Despite these wartime assurances, it was widely anticipated that a prolonged depression, like that into which the economy had plunged shortly after the first world war, would recur soon after the ending of the second. The post-war recovery proved not merely temporary as that of 1918 had been, however, but persisted, though with much faltering, into the long boom. Overall unemployment averaged little more than 1.5 per cent until the end of the 1960s, exceeding the apparently wildly optimistic expectations of Beveridge during the war when he said that if unemployment could be kept down to 3 per cent the country would be doing very well. The regional unemployment that had characterized the 1930s persisted in rates of 2.8 per cent and 3.4 per cent in the North and in Scotland, while in Northern Ireland unemployment has never been less than 7 per cent. In Glasgow, for instance, half of all fourteen-year-old boys leaving school in 1947 were unemployed for some time during the next three years. In part this was due to frequent job changing. For although most school leavers were clear about what they wanted to do, with skilled manual work being the most popular choice and half of them obtaining apprenticeships, '. . . aimless shifting from job to job is still characteristic of 1 boy in 4' (Ferguson & Cunnison 1952: 54).

However, the information yielded by such surveys gave little support to the idea that there was an almost caste-like system in industrial grades of labour. 'The weight of evidence goes to show that the occupational status of the father has had little influence on the son, whether in respect to the job-preference he expressed on leaving school or to the actual status he held at the age of 17' (ibid.: 41). Indeed, economic changes allowed for almost doubling the numbers required for non-manual occupations and for skilled manual work. The numbers of sons compared with fathers in unskilled work also increased post-war, with a decrease in the intermediate semi-skilled category, though it is unclear how these terms were defined exactly.

In conformity with Freestone's (1939) suggestion that children tend to aim at the highest levels available to the group to which they belong, Liversidge (1962) found that assignment to a grammar school elevated the aspirations of working-class children while assignment to a secondary modern tended to depress the aspirations of middle-class boys. The exception to this rule was the continued high expectations of secondary modern girls, possibly because of the clerical and office work becoming available to many of them. Older girls were found to aspire higher than younger, determined as they were to avoid 'dirty' factory work and other manual work considered unfeminine. 'The general picture which emerges from this study is one of startlingly accurate appraisal of life chances by the children, and a shrewd appreciation of the social and economic implications of their placing within the educational system. They know at what age they will marry, the best type of job they can get, and the best wage they can hope to earn in that job. Having accepted the role that they are to play in life, they rarely venture out of it even in fantasy' (ibid.: 74). Like others, Liversidge had divided his questions as to future occupations into 'reality' and 'fantasy' choices, but was surprised to find little difference between them.

Whatever the climate of opinion among parents and pupils, the major concern of liberal thought and social democratic policy was with equal access to the new system of schooling. The dominant model of education was a 'contest' or race in which the starting point of all the contestants was to be progressively equalized so as to give each an equal chance of attaining whatever goal their ambitions and interests selected from the limited number available. In conception the system was intended as one of meritocracy. It was supposed, like the Chinese system for the education of mandarins, to promote the ablest minds, irrespective of their class of origin, to the service of industry and the state. This would prevent the 'waste of talent' in the working class that was so often commented upon. This model could be contrasted with a 'sponsorship' system in which, as in the private preparatory and public schools, there was special preparation for elite status for a limited number who were early segregated from their fellows (Turner 1964).

By raising the age of special selection to eleven, the post-war settlement was still a mixture of contest and sponsorship models. The logic of its development for further progressive reform, however, was to raise the age at which selection took place and thus avoid any segregation until the late stages, as in the US system. It was assumed that if 'access' and 'opportunities' – the terms in which the problem of opening education to the working class was conceived – were improved and working-class children were enabled to achieve educationally, then society would gradually become more egalitarian. Antique class divisions would dissolve in a sea of affluence and prosperity, so that the working class could actually be educated out of existence.

Critics of tripartite schooling

For the criticism that was made of the tripartite system was that it did not work as a means of meritocratic selection. Rather, it reinforced already existing class divisions in society. This view was expressed by a progressive section within the Labour Party which gradually came to dominance over those favouring the traditional virtues of grammar schooling for bright working-class children. They were supported by a specialist group of intellectuals from the relatively new discipline of the sociology of education and the teachers' unions. These three forces, as Madan Sarup says (1982: 59) 'largely shaped education in post-war Britain'. The National Union of Teachers especially enjoyed 'a cosy symbiotic relationship' with the Department of Education and Science 'from the 1944 Act until the Great Debate of the 1970s, when the NUT's national influence began to wane' (Dale 1983: 40).

The criticism of tripartitism was bluntly put in class terms. This was unusual at a time when Marxism had yet to be accepted on equal terms as a competing school of thought in the plural society of academia. Then 'The word "class" ', as Tawney put it, was still 'fraught with unpleasing associations, so that to linger upon it is apt to be interpreted as the symptom of a perverted mind and a jaundiced spirit' (quoted in Marwick 1980: 7). However, the definition of class adopted was either the Registrar General's five-class schema, which had originated in 1911 for the purpose of a comparative study of infant mortality, or the refinement of it by Moser and Hall (1954) to produce a more precise seven-point scale, or some further refinement of that. Definition was thus reified in terms of status and not of power. Also, these measures of the social status of the various occupations of pupils' fathers were assumed to be static indicators of a settled social situation, rather than one subject to increasing economic and technological change. There was also the tendency, already noted, for the upper or ruling class to disappear from these taxonomies as studies were limited to the state system. In addition, within the state schools definition became circular so that the working class was defined as those who did badly at school and those who did badly at school were defined as working class.

Young and Whitty remarked the 'obsession' of 'policy makers – particularly those in Labour administrations – and their academic advisers . . . during the past thirty years or so with the problem of working-class failure at school'. They showed that 'the problem' then became 'to identify correlations between cultural features of working-class life and failure at school – factors which then became "deficiencies" for which educational policy makers attempted to devise programmes of compensation' (1977: 3–4). 'This approach was based on several unquestioned assumptions: that schooling as currently practised was good, that selection was a prime function of education, that talent and merit could be identified objectively as traits of individuals, so that individual mobility in education demonstrated that greater equality of opportunity was being achieved' (Meighan 1981: 327).

Official concern with those failing to take advantage of the opportunities to access provided by the new system was first recorded by the Ministry of Education's 1954 Report *Early*

Leavers. This was a proportion of the school population to which official concern was to return repeatedly. It comprised, in a phrase from an editorial in *The Times* that can only be compared for its elegant circumlocution with the delicate phrasing of Sir Ian, '. . . that section of the public that has no hope or ambition of becoming thrusting executives . . .'(17/9/75). As the Report concluded: 'We have been impressed above all with the far-reaching influence of a child's home background.' So that '. . . a quarter of the children of unskilled workers were capable of some kind of sixth form work compared with the 6.7 per cent who are getting it' (HMSO 1954: 56, 20). These pupils were considered not only to have wasted their own personal opportunities to advance their positions in society, but also as themselves a wasted national resource that was not being fully exploited.

As well as this major focus of official concern there was the first of a number of charges, repeated with each reorganization of the education system, that the new arrangements were failing to inculcate basic literacy and numeracy, through the revelation of the low standards of recruits for the Korean war (Lewis 1955). There was also the associated worry, voiced, for instance, by Hoggart (1958), that the new 'American' popular culture of the mass media was undermining and debasing the traditional, healthy values of the working class. This was linked to an older and essentially elitist advocacy of the need to preserve 'higher' culture against the cheapening effects of mass production (e.g. Leavis and Thompson 1942). The problem was among the most apparently pressing facing educationalists in the new age of affluence which seemed such a contrast with remembered pre-war poverty. As Coates and Silburn stated, 'During the fifties the myth that widespread material poverty had been finally and triumphantly overcome was so universally current, so widely accepted by politicians, social commentators and the general public alike, that for a decade and more, public controversy and political discussion were engrossed by the new (and fundamentally more encouraging) problems of what people are still pleased to call the "Affluent Society"' (1970: 13).

Nowadays it is hard to imagine the widespread existence

of such an illusion. However, for social scientists, administrators and their wider public it was not finally dispelled until the publication in 1965 of Abel-Smith and Townsend's *The Poor and the Poorest*. This showed that the proportion of the population living within the official definition of poverty had doubled between 1953 and 1960 to 7.5 million. Before this it was the accepted and general belief that the welfare state had abolished poverty and that it hung on in a few insalubrious areas that would soon be redeveloped and cleared up. In Liverpool's dockside, for instance, Mays (1962) observed an introverted, bottle-smashing community at odds with the local schools. The general picture of this 'inner urban area', as Mays called it, was of an exceptional and aberrant group whose shared subculture was the main obstacle to their children's progress to social improvement.

20:40:40

The Crowther Report indicated the economic basis for this cultural blockage in its finding that early leaving from grammar schools was 'negligible if the father's income exceeded £16 a week' (HMSO 1959: 19). Again, the raising of the school-leaving age was recommended with extended courses for all secondary modern pupils. This was seen as part of a broadening of the tripartite system, expanding the secondary technical schools to train 'the technicians and craftsmen of the future' (34). Such training was not deemed appropriate for girls, maturing through ever earlier adolescence so that '. . . marriage now looms larger and nearer in the pupils' eyes than it ever has before.' If girls were to be encouraged to go into the fifth year and sixth forms they would have to be attracted by courses in suitable vocational skills: '. . . shorthand, typing, and in some schools, accounts' (para. 457). Encouraging teachers with expectations of professional and financial improvements, Crowther urged them to 'experiment' in the 'no man's land between school and work' (para. 197). These suggestions for technical and vocational education were not to be taken up for some time. More immediately, Crowther laid the foundation for regularizing the examination system. GCE O levels, instituted in 1951, were designed for the top 20 per cent of the school population and could only be taken by them at age sixteen, one year above the still statutory leaving age. Now Crowther advised the development of CSE for the next third of the population regarded as examinable.

'As is obvious from a description of these examinations, a substantial proportion of pupils leave school without having entered for either GCE or CSE' (Rutter *et al.* 1979: 39). Consequently, as has been much noted recently, secondary schools fail the majority of their pupils. For those seeking further social democratic advance towards greater egalitarianism, this is an argument for a unitary, equal exam for all 'to have a go at', however unequal their preparation for it. The Schools Council first suggested such a merger in 1970 and the NUT before that. Again, it is ironic that it was a Conservative government which eventually introduced a unitary GCSE. Although, as Sir Keith Joseph made clear, 'distinction' and 'merit' grades would still signal suitability for higher education as O levels indicated it before. (GCSE passes are in fact graded from A to G, ABC being O level equivalent while F corresponds to the average majority pass of CSE grade 4. There are more or less subtle methods of differentiation which vary from subject to subject and board to board. In some there are separate papers for the various grades, or extension papers for the top grades. In maths there is an incline of difficulty in the questions set and different levels of marking. In English 'teacher guidance' is necessary for candidates to select 'appropriate tasks'.)

For the majority of pupils their relegation to the second best CSE or no exam at all reinforced their feelings of worthlessness compared with those taking the higher exams. The division of labour between manual and mental, 'thick' and 'brainy' was thus perpetuated. Crowther did not think that the majority of children should be 'subjected to external examination' at all; they were better taught 'a sensible practicality', 'moral standards' and 'a wise use of leisure time'. Thus nearly half of all pupils were to become the 'below average children' of Newsom's concern (1963a). Meanwhile, the familiar pattern of 20:40:40 – 20 per cent O level: 40 per cent CSE: 40 per cent low-grade CSE/fail/non-exam – began to establish itself as the first CSEs were taken in 1965.

In graphic form, examination certificates vary inversely with employment opportunities. A situation of full employment corresponds with low or no certification, while the ideal opposite of full unemployment would, were it possible, correspond with universal certification (a situation that seems to be approaching with the 1990s!). So this major expansion of examination certification coincided with the first apparent falterings of the economy after the 'long boom' since the war. It is noticeable that examination inflation, or diploma devaluation as it was called in the States, occurs not at a time when the economy is expanding and jobs are plentiful, but as the economy contracts and jobs become scarce. It is then that validation by the education system is called into question. When employees are in demand neither employers, parents nor pupils worry too much about their qualifications for the job. On this model, the extension of examination to the 'next quartile' through the CSE served to certificate applicants for apprenticeships to skilled trades that were to become increasingly scarce through the continuous application of new technology. Numbers of apprentices peaked in 1966, though the proportion of young workers apprenticed did not decline until its highest 25 per cent in 1969 (FECRDU 1980: 34–5).

Setting up a new examination system was not the main motivation of Crowther's committee however. 'Anxieties about the effects of the "bulge" on the juvenile labour market (and also about the "wastage" of talent from early school leaving), formed the basis for the Crowther recommendations' (Reeder 1979: 138). Wastage of talent is the main theme of Jackson and Marsden's classic 1962 chronicle of the cultural pressure upon the chosen few working-class pupils, whose drop-out rate from grammar school after O level (72 per cent and 85 per cent, compared with 38 per cent of middle-class pupils, as recorded by Crowther) stimulated their investigation. The 88 working-class children traced by them formed a minority within 'Marburton's' grammar schools. The history of their conflicting experience with '. . . the school's determination to hand on the grammar school modes, to spread its standards as the best and only standards, and the child's clumsy, awkward and stubborn desire to preserve the other ways, to remain "natural" '(Jackson and

Marsden 1962: 111) forms the substance of the book. It recorded also the growing estrangement between parents and their successful child and the lack of communication between parents and schools. In summary, 'The children who lasted the full grammar school course came from the upper strata of the working class' (152). But the authors also introduced the notion of a 'sunken middle-class' and reinforced Hoggart's idea of the importance of a 'pushing' mother, whose literary type seems to be Mrs Morel in Lawrence's *Sons and Lovers*.

Both these notions have since been questioned on statistical evidence by Halsey (1980: 88–9). But earlier literacy and smaller families, as well as differences in housing, have been repeatedly identified as disposing a working-class child to success in a middle-class orientated system; the lack of them in the majority insuring their failure. Although success for the persevering was not without price, '. . . most of the 88 completed their education happily and successfully.' 'They are now middle-class citizens' (Jackson and Marsden 1962: 153). The system was thus self-perpetuating. As a system of meritocracy it was only partially successful and it was not designed as a system of equalization. In fact, Jackson and Marsden considered that the secondary modern, grammar and public schools served only to reinforce the trisection of English society into working, middle and upper classes. The problem thus remained: 'How can we open education to the working class?' (211).

A short essay by Webb in the *British Journal of Sociology* for 1962 gave a pungent flavour of what went on in a secondary modern school of the type to which the majority of the working class were confined. First, 'Hostility (between teachers and boys) is the key factor at Black School.' This hostility, 'ranging from the mild to the ferocious', amounted to 'almost a guerilla war against the teacher's standards – a ragged, intermittent fight to be oneself by being spontaneous and irrepressible and by breaking rules.' The analogy of sergeant and drill squad described the teaching relationship at Black School, with the corollary that only the most mechanical tasks could be taught there. The 'obsession' of the teachers with control over their classes helped to answer the question: 'How does this school, apparently such an anachronism, survive in this day and age? On the boys' side it survives because the drill-sergeant method fits quite harmoniously (as no other method would) into the context of the school. And it survives also, on the boys' side, because informally it is in harmony with the street gang, and with the boy's job later, which typically is semi-skilled and tedious. On the teachers' side, it survives because the staff ideology (hate, fear, fatigue) make for an aversion against thinking more than is absolutely necessary about the job.'

Because conditions have remained unchanged, job prospects being still – if not increasingly – semi-skilled and tedious, the recurrent demand for a return to such traditional discipline in schools always finds a resonance with many parents. Drill-sergeant methods fitted the context of many schools more 'harmoniously' than the methods that came, in different degrees, to replace them. For Holly, such contradictions show the profound divisions within society and the futility of attempting to resolve them within a unitary education system. 'In the traditional situation of the "tough" secondary modern school, legitimated by generations of expectation based on familial experience, coercion is seen by all as inevitable. . . . In the new situation of the urban comprehensive, with a growing complement of graduate teachers originally destined for the academic sector, and an element of would-be academic students, coercion comes to be resented by students. . . . At the same time it becomes a bone of contention among teachers. They are faced with attempting to unify what is, in fact, not unifiable – social relations of education relevant to routine workers with those relevant to managerial/technological workers' (1977: 186–7).

The effects of selection

It is often alleged that comprehensive schools 'failed' bright working-class children, where grammar schools and streamed selection promoted individual talent. To prove this an historical approach would have to be adopted. The achievement of the grammar schools in a particular area would have to be taken together with the record of all the secondary moderns there in order to compare this total picture with the present performance of all the area's comprehensives. Such a comparison in a given locality has never been attempted and would be difficult if not impossible, since so many other factors, not only the change in education system, have to be taken into account. Reynolds and Sullivan's (1987) local comparison of two Welsh areas, one comprehensive and the other selective, is too small a sample to be representative. Between areas with different systems, the National Child Development Study, which followed a sample of 16,000 born in one week of March 1958, is the most complete assessment of the comprehensive experiment nationally. The comforting academic consensus, for example in the conclusion to the latest report from the Study, is that academically orientated children have succeeded as well in the comprehensives as in the grammar schools, but for the average child progress in comprehensives is the same as it was in the secondary moderns (Stedman 1980: 16–19). This same result may have been achieved because the changes have not been as fundamental as they appear, or because the same selective ends are now attained by different means.

The effects of selection at eleven-plus upon the primary level below was the subject of Jackson's next investigation following his collaboration with Marsden. As a teacher in a streamed primary school, Jackson saw the pressures of individual selection extending downwards into primary schools to make them 'an education system in miniature'. He proposed that the existence of selective mechanisms in the tier above reproduced streamed situations in the supposedly undifferentiated layer below. Selective pressures worked upon and heightened the social differentiation produced by the child's home and class background. These familial factors produced what Jackson called a condition of 'learning readiness', cultivated in these very young children '. . . by many people from fellow teachers, to parents and even grandparents, and the schools, colleges and teachers they had known long ago' (1964: 2). He thus anticipated the notion of 'cultural capital' which was later used to explain in part the failings of comprehensive secondaries. For Jackson though, these factors were not the exclusive product of education but were also engendered by the whole tendency of modern capitalist society, so that 'Even if streaming as we know it came to an end, it seems likely that this mesh of values would continually produce other systems and devices with the same effects' (13).

To those advocates of further progressive reform towards class equalization, raising the age of selection appeared as the next step in the social democratic programme for education. Indeed to Halsey such an evolution had an historic inevitability: 'The development of education in Western industrialized countries may be summarized as having characteristically three stages. In the first stage primary education is universalized and is terminal for the majority with a minority going on to secondary and tertiary education. In the second stage secondary education is universalized, the primary schools are transitional to the secondary schools and a minority go on to tertiary institutions. In the third stage the secondary schools become transitional to a system of mass higher education . . .' (Halsey 1980: 24). The universities, and Oxbridge preeminently, those bastions of class power and privilege, were thus the next target for further reform. As Bernstein put it (1971: 190), 'The condition for a major shift in the knowledge code at the secondary level is a major shift in the knowledge code at the tertiary level.' But first the step of raising the age of selection and opening the secondary schools to give a supposedly equal chance to all of continuing higher education had to be taken as part of a political programme of continuing social change.

The research evidence that had accumulated throughout the fifties and early sixties centred upon the relation of social class to academic achievement. Typical of these studies was Halsey, Floud and Martin's 1965 *Social Class and Educational Opportunity*. This compared Hertfordshire with Middlesbrough to show that in the former, where 'virtually everyone enjoys an adequate basic income and good housing' (89), eleven-plus success depended upon family size and the education and attitudes of parents and not on the material environment of the home. In the North, where incomes and housing standards were lower, 'the successful children at each social level were distinguished by the relative material prosperity of their homes' (145). With the rise in material standards the remaining problem blocking the educational advance of the working class thus appeared to be one of culture and attitudes.

Official government recognition that working-class children were not advancing as they should through the new opportunities opened by the 1944 Education Act came in the Robbins Report on Higher Education. In an appendix it acknowledged that 'Children with fathers in professional and managerial occupations are twenty times more likely to enter full-time higher education than are those with fathers in semi- and un-skilled jobs. The differences are again much greater for girls than for boys' (HMSO 1963b: 38). Despite the increase in numbers of undergraduates since the war, proportions recruited from the various social classes remained unaltered. Authority now recognized what critics had alleged, that as Sarup summarized, '. . . a class-based system, with the public schools at the top and the secondary modern schools at the bottom, had survived the social upheaval of the post-war years largely intact' (1982: 9). For, although 'It is sometimes imagined that the increase in recent years in the numbers achieving good school-leaving qualifications has occurred almost entirely among the children of manual workers. This is not so' (Robbins 1963b: 53). So the 'pool of ability' in the working class lay still untapped, while the smaller but presumably proportionally the same 'pool' in the professional and managerial classes, which might have been thought to have been quite dried up, had proved capable of elastic expansion. This untapped national asset must, the Report urged, be realized by an expansion of higher education: 'For the production of trained manpower is like the production of long lived capital goods'; and 'There is a broad connection between the size of the stock of trained manpower in a community and its level of productivity per head' (ibid.: 70).

Examination inflation

In the same year as Robbins dealt with those advancing to higher education, Newsom concentrated on 'below average children', the 'Browns' and the 'Robinsons' as his report called them (HMSO 1963a). Like Crowther, Newsam advised raising the school-leaving age with the last year spent partly off site in FE colleges and on work experience. This should be part of a general relating of learning in the last years at school to employment and an outgoing programme of initiation to the adult world of work and leisure linked with the (then) Youth Employment Service. Like Robbins, Newsom initiated a general expansion in new buildings and equipment – £300 million a year throughout the 1960s. Positive discrimination in the way of extra resources for impoverished areas advanced a policy of Educational Priority Areas under a different name. A 'core curriculum', though not in so many words, of raising numeracy and literacy standards was also advised. But Newsam specifically enjoined these new schools to resist pressures to extend the new public examinations to those pupils for whom they were inappropriate. Rather all leavers should receive a leaving certificate combining assessment and a general school record. In fact, just the opposite happened, most leavers being certified by schools solely in terms of exams they may or may not have passed.

Parental attitudes to examinations are complicated by those 'normative patterns of social aspiration' to which was attributed the cultural blockage restraining working-class children in the new education system. Exams are generally accepted as the passport to 'escape'. The pride which even comprehensives take in their examination and sixth-form successes, a tendency heightened by the Thatcher government's insistence upon the publication of examination results, contains the 'hidden curricular' message that 'There is something wrong with being, and certainly with ending up as being, working class. To be working class is something unfortunate and undesirable from which any pupil with any sense will seek to escape' (Hargreaves 1978: 52). But, as Jackson and Marsden showed, even parents committed to their children 'getting on' often felt ambivalent about their children becoming 'better' than themselves.

How much parents and children remain committed to the ideology of social mobility through education and how much they are open to the suggestion that in times of economic stringency their children are best taught 'practical' and 'useful' skills will determine how much parents support teachers' efforts to motivate pupils to work for exams. They may continue to wave with them the carrot of 'study-hard-to-get-a-good-job', seeing this as even more important when jobs are scarce. Or they may accept the vocational curriculum of profile-accredited, criterion-referenced, work-derived tasks. But even if exams no longer guarantee access to jobs, they remain the route to higher education, although, even here, as Black (1980) has reviewed the literature to show, they are poorly predictive of future academic success. A Schools Council investigation similarly found that by the nature of the marking and standardization system, one quarter of O level and CSE candidates are given the wrong grades and that the chances of substantially improving this inconsistency are remote (Wilmott and Nuttall 1975).

There are many explanations of why secondary schooling became wholly given over to certification by examination. For those who follow the theories of the German sociologist Max Weber, this is a natural consequence of modern society's increasing bureaucratization. An equally natural process was widely assumed at the time in the developing economy, which supposedly generated more demanding technical and scientific jobs, requiring the attestation of ever higher standards of competence. Banks in a standard work, for example, asserted that 'One of the main features of a modern industrial society is the extent to which entry to a large range of occupations is increasingly dependent on the acquisition of the necessary educational qualifications' (1968: 201). However, the coincidence of the extension of examinations to the next quartile (below the top 20 per cent) with changes in the labour market tending to a decline in the number of skilled jobs without the creation of numerous scientific and technical jobs requiring new skills, has already been noted.

One reason for the extension of examinations was that the new comprehensives felt the need to compete with the established grammar schools on their own terms of academic success. The collapse of the tripartite system of grammar, secondary modern and technical schools into comprehensives resulted in a loss of technical education, which Halsey regarded as '. . . one of the tragedies of British education after the second war' (1980: 214). Reasons for this tragedy may again be related to changing demands for skilled labour. The general demand that had been anticipated did not occur and so such specialized technical training as was required occurred in colleges of Further Education, while technical departments were absorbed into comprehensives where training played a subordinate role to the more academic education to which the new schools aspired.

Employers have also been blamed for increasingly linking occupational rewards to educational qualifications. 'Employers want a convenient method of sorting out suitable applicants for jobs; a paper qualification obtained by examination is one such method, and hence the school curriculum often tends to be treated simply as a means to examination success' (Parker 1977: 35). Symptoms of this 'Diploma Disease' according to Dore (1976) are that when too many applicants chase too few top jobs employers raise the qualification requirements. Applicants who no longer qualify for those jobs then apply for the next jobs down. Soon only those with qualifications previously required for top jobs can get the next to top ones and so on down the line to the bottom of the heap where the unqualified get squeezed out.

However the 'convenience' of exams for employers is acknowledged to be at odds with the 'common sense' notion that academic success does not predict practical ability or future progress at work. This was substantiated by Berg (1971) in the US and Cherry (1980) in the UK. Moreover, examination inflation seems restricted to a section of managerial and professional occupations. Employers, repeated studies have shown, even in times of high unemployment, prefer to use their established procedures for recruiting skilled and (increasingly) semi- and unskilled labour. Here exam results and school reports count less than personal attitudes and are used, if at all, merely to screen for initial selection of candidates.

To take two of many studies, Ashton and Maguire, reporting in a letter to *The Times* (23/6/81) their findings from interviewing a representative sample of 350 employers in three contrasted labour markets, stated that: 'In recruitment to a wide range of occupations, including many in the white-collar and skilled manual sectors, employers attach greater importance to "personal skills and qualities" than to academic qualifications. This was frequently true even when such qualifications were stipulated as a requirement for entry to a particular job.' Thus, 'Our results would indicate that it is the educationalists who tend to overemphasize the importance of qualifications. Employers are much more sceptical of their value.' And Cuming's (1983) investigation of the attitudes of Leicestershire employers, parents and pupils also confirmed that: 'Parental and student expectations of the importance of examinations in recruitment to work are very high. In comparison, employers' actual use of qualifications is low' (Abstract).

Although Cuming agrees with the general finding that unqualified school leavers are more likely to be unemployed than qualified, he disagrees that this is because they are academically unqualified: '. . . applicants with basic skills and the "right attitudes to work" who are otherwise not academically inclined will only be at a disadvantage if they are made to think that they are or, worse, are persuaded to take examinations which are as unsuited to their interests and abilities as they are to employers' needs' (61–2). The exact 'needs' of employers and 'the right attitudes to work' are rather difficult to establish, however, since, as Finn (1982: 44) said, 'They [employers] are more concerned with the general, social dispositions and characteristics of their workers than with their particular abilities to carry out specific technical tasks. Hence their demands are usually extremely vague, calling, for example, for workers with the ability to "learn to learn" and to "adapt and change".'

Responsibility for expanding and further refining the examination system in the change-over from the tripartite to the comprehensive system can be ascribed mainly to teachers and educational administrators. For initially, as Durkheim outlined in *The Evolution of Educational Thought*, it is only the educational system itself that is concerned with examination results as a certification of competence for higher education. This type of examination presupposes the existence of university institutions with an organized body of professional teachers providing for their own perpetuation. In addition, 'A course syllabus based on paper qualifications dictates the knowledge needed for the students, obviating, even ruling against, thinking clearly and immediately about what kind of learning and teaching would be relevant for that student, although the standard curriculum's relevance is questioned by parties on all sides' (Hill and Scharff 1976: 300–1). Teachers are thus blamed for inflicting upon their pupils an education identical with their own, which left them only with the skill of passing examinations. Certainly examinations were extended by teachers throughout the new comprehensive schools largely as a means of control and management over a school population no longer separated into three different types of school.

CHAPTER 3

The comprehensive solution (1964–1976)

Labour's comprehensive policy

Limited comprehensive experiments began under Conservative administrations in the 1950s, but the wholesale introduction of comprehensive schooling followed the election of Wilson's Labour government in 1964. During its long opposition Labour had not at first been driven to consider any new initiative following its post-war 'settlement' of education. When education was eventually again placed upon the agenda, the necessary reform was conceived in terms of the wastage of national talent revealed by Crowther and Robbins and as a means of lessening class antagonism and increasing social cohesion. Crosland (1956: 147) argued that 'We cannot be content with correctly distributing all the (as it were) alpha material, but must make best use of our beta resources also.' Thus 'division into streams of ability' remained essential, as Roy Jenkins made clear when he stressed that although a comprehensive would 'include within its intake children now classified into the different types of grammar, technical and secondary modern. It does not imply that these children will be taught in the same classes and all do the same work. They must be divided according to intelligence and aptitude . . . but the divisions will be less sharp and less final' (1959: 96).

Despite Wilson's depreciations of the 'educational apartheid' of the eleven-plus, it was a softening rather than an abolition of selection that was intended. Wilson also reassured teachers just before the 1964 election that grammar schools would be abolished over his dead body (Kogan 1975: 219–20). Typically, he offered something for everybody: industrialists were told reformed schools would provide the skilled workforce for modernization and growth, while working-class voters were promised education would overcome the unequal opportunities created by class divisions. Since selection at eleven-plus was discredited and unpopular but grammar schools retained their high status and general respect, Wilson could have it both ways by presenting comprehensive schools as 'grammar school education for all'. As in any two-party contest by direct election, the secret of success lay in winning over the middle block of voters. 'By marginally widening the opportunities for upward social mobility . . . the expansion of higher education . . . appealed to a social class group who form part of the natural constituency of the Tory Party' (Harris 1983: 50). The middle class found they could forget the trauma of the eleven-plus, which was unpredictable in its rejection of more children than it selected, and that self-selection by residential neighbourhood was a far more congenial arrangement. Meanwhile the public schools were left outside the scope of reform, so that what Crosland had considered 'absurd from a socialist point of view' actually occurred: '. . . to close down the grammar schools while leaving the public schools still holding their present commanding position' (1956: 275).

The Labour Party as a whole for long remained ambivalent in its support for comprehensive reform. Since the advocates of independent working-class education had failed to find a foothold in the party, Labour had remained committed to an extension of working-class opportunities within the existing system. This meant free, fair and competitive access to secondaries with the grammar school as the paradigm of excellence. Many older members of local ruling Labour groups were anti-comprehensive, while the party as a whole was unenthusiastic. There were consequently delays in plans for comprehensive reorganization, even when Labour was in government. Rubinstein and Simon (1973: 110) record that when Labour left office in 1970 only 12 per cent of secondary pupils attended 'genuinely' comprehensive schools, most of the changes having been in name only, redesignating secondary moderns as comprehensives.

According to the 'Statistics of Education' 1979, 'A School is classified as comprehensive when its admission arrangements are without reference to ability and aptitude.' DES Circular 10/65 stated, 'A comprehensive school aims to establish a school community in which pupils cover the whole ability range and with differing interests and backgrounds can be encouraged to mix with each other, gaining stimulus from the contacts and learning tolerance and understanding in the process' (para. 36). This was 'the social case' for comprehensive schools which Shirley Williams still considers 'unanswerable . . . educating children of different backgrounds and of different abilities together . . . to break down class barriers and the mutual ignorance of different social groups, and create the context for a more democratic, open and unprejudiced society' (1981: 156). The impossible project of social democratic policy was never stated more clearly, though Neil Kinnock continues to repeat it, referring to schools as 'the solvent of class division and personal disadvantage' (*New Socialist* 3–4/86), while 'Labour's Programme 1982' talked of education as the 'main instrument' in 'equalizing . . . the social distribution of life chances'. But for Mrs Williams, by 1977 the process was already complete for '. . . in three quarters of our schools the selective system is a thing of the past' (HMSO 1977: 1). Even if this were true, the superimposition of formal equality of provision in neighbourhoods differentiated on the basis of class residence offered no more real equality than free milk from Hoxton to Harrow.

By 1970 Benn and Simon reckoned they were 'Half Way There'. But, in terms of sex alone, although less than one-third of all state schools were now single sex, half the schools they surveyed restricted some subjects to boys or girls only, while nearly all mixed secondaries (98 per cent) separated the sexes at some point before sixteen. In terms of mixed ability, only 22 per cent of the schools surveyed grouped first-year children in this way and only 4 per cent continued it in a complete system of non-streamed classes; while two-thirds of the schools had no mixed-ability groups at all. Mixed ability tended to be confined to such subjects as Art and Games. London Inspectors had already dismissed the idea of 'teaching groups covering the whole range of ability' as 'impractical' (LCC 1961: 32). But, as Benn and Simon indicated, 'The practice of strict streaming . . . is . . . clearly incompatible with genuine comprehensive reorganisation in the long run' (1970: 360).

Marsden, asking 'Which Comprehensive Principle?' (1969: 2–5), saw the danger 'that the appearance of change to comprehensives, like the 1944 Butler Reforms, will remove the pressure for real change, effectively preserving selective education and making the achievement of non-selective, truly comprehensive education less likely.' He urged new forms of assessment to break the bottleneck which highly selective examination for higher education imposed upon the secondary sector. But Young, writing earlier in the same journal (1967: 6–11), had already argued that even if higher education were open to all secondary pupils, the universities would only adopt the same 'cooling out' strategies that they used in the USA. He argued that comprehensivization could not be achieved until the link between educational attainment and occupational status was broken.

As a reaction to the reorganization of secondary schooling and to changes in primaries following the Plowden Report, argument again began over a defence of standards. As Halsey, Heath and Ridge said, 'To claim that standards have declined may be a plea that certain kinds of traditional knowledge ought to be valued' (1980: 111). The Black Papers began making that plea from 1969 onwards with a defence of academic excellence drawn in debased form from the tradition of conservative cultural criticism that runs from Arnold to Leavis. They also drew upon the discredited psychology of Sir Cyril Burt to treat social inequalities as natural differences.

The argument runs and runs, for instance over the latest report of the National Children's Bureau on their cohort of 11,000 children. In its first published form in 1980 the report showed no statistical difference between the attainment of pupils in the grammar/secondary modern system and in comprehensives, once allowance had been made for social class. But after the intervention by right-wing educationalists associated with the (then) junior education minister, Rhodes Boyson, the report was republished with unadjusted, raw scores which have been taken to demonstrate the superiority of the selective system (as Marks and Srzednicki 1985). This clearly shows the way in which apparently purely academic disputes provide the basis for government concern and intervention, even when government chooses to act on only one side of the argument and ignores the weight of academic opinion.

An even clearer case was the research of Start and Wells claiming to have found that 'The Trend of Reading Standards' (1972) was a downward one. This prompted Mrs Thatcher as Minister of Education to appoint Lord Bullock to head a committee of inquiry; this, despite the doubt that was quickly cast upon the validity of the research findings. For Start and Wells's sample of schools had been much reduced by 73 per cent of their primary schools refusing to cooperate with them and their losing 47 per cent of the data from their secondaries during the postal strike. Another 9 per cent of the design sample was lost through an 'office mishap'. The reading tests they administered were over twenty years old and no account was taken of the effects of immigration in their results. Above all, the 'drop' in reading standards which was made so much of was not an absolute one. It was the difference between the improvement that had been anticipated on the basis of the previous rise in standards and the standard actually achieved. In a review of six surveys of reading standards, including Start and Wells, Burke and Lewis (1974–5) summarized: 'No justification was found for a belief that standards are declining.' Reading standards overall are relative, as Bullock noted. 'It is obvious that as society becomes more complex and makes higher demands in awareness and understanding of its members the criteria of literacy will rise' (HMSO 1975: 11). It is not so obvious that society is making such higher demands upon those it consigns to the dole or to jobs which are, increasingly, routinized and deskilled and require no, or minimal, literacy. (One in four adults in Britain today take *The Sun*, a newspaper with an average reading age of eight.)

The sociology of the new education

Throughout the 1960s spending on education rose to surpass that for defence for the first time in 1969. Yet at the end of this period of expansion the Council for Educational Advance pointed out that three in four primary school buildings were substandard and one in two secondaries. The expansion at all levels, except adult education, allowed a growth in teacher training and, linked to it, the establishment of the sociology of education as a discrete discipline within social science. The previous statistical studies of 'life chances' for individuals from different classes had been undertaken by sociologists who did not conceive of education as their particular field of study. They had demonstrated the inequality of selection to different levels of education upon the basis of a spread of ability revealed by intelligence testing. This notion of innate intelligence had been replaced in the Crowther, Newsom and Plowden Reports with ideas of interest and needs requiring development. The problems of equalizing chances for educational selection were thus posed in a new way in the new system. The sociology of education now made its own an explication of these problems and their proposed solution in terms of the reform of education then in progress. As Young and Whitty summarized: 'The sociological research largely complemented the public reports and was tacitly accepted as a basis for an expansionist policy by successive ministers' (1977: 20).

Material standards and educational expenditure were rising, therefore the problem of opening education to the working class was no longer perceived as one of economic poverty. Rather, traditional attitudes and culture, even language, were the brake upon more of the workers' children taking advantage of the new opportunities to rise to the skilled and scientific responsibilities of the technological revolution. The remedies suggested by sociologists of education for this problem became increasingly radical. Cultural, or subcultural, studies were translated from the USA where, similarly, notions of inherited intelligence had been largely rejected as explanations of the failure of blacks particularly to advance in a mobile and competitive society. They had also been applied to studies of teenagers, youths and gangs.

Downes in Poplar and Stepney did not discover a US-type delinquency. Instead of 'alienation' induced by 'status frustration', he found 'dissociation' from the dominant values of school and society and a 'reaffirmation of traditional working-class values' (1966: 258). Thus there was '. . . an opting out of the joint middle- and skilled working-class value system'; so that '. . . the adolescent in a "dead-end" job, in a "dead-end" neighbourhood, extricates himself from the belief in work as of any importance beyond the single provision of income, and deflects what aspirations he has left into areas of what has been termed "non-work" ' (235–6). Wilmott, returning at the same time as Downes to Bethnal Green to interview 'Adolescent Boys in East London', gives a similar account of 'ordinary youths', all of whom could be defined as delinquent, since, as with Downes, 'Stealing, it seems, is part of the "normal" behaviour of boys in Bethnal Green, as it is apparently in other working-class areas.' To these ordinary youths their schools, all of which seemed 'in greater or lesser degree, out of tune with the local community', were 'at best irrelevant and at worst an irritant' (1966: 140 and 99).

It was long before sociologists of education could attain this level of objectivity. When, as Corrigan (1979: 21) recorded, 'deviancy theories became transferred to the sociology of education in the late 1960s', their application was from within the schools and committed to their values, trying to make the new comprehensives work instead of finding out why they were not working. In addition, educational sociology, in initially drawing up the boundaries of its discipline, restricted itself to what happens within schools. It isolated them from the wider society, following an inclination shared by many teachers. 'For a long time it has been almost a professional disease among educators to regard school education as though it operated in a social vacuum and to disregard the incompatibilities between school and society' (Husen 1972: 156). Hargreaves (1967) and Lacey (1970) in a Manchester secondary modern and grammar school respectively, typify this intensive study of single schools. Both found that streaming within the schools reinforced the peer group values of their boys and that this differentiation was accentuated by the production of values in the lower streams which were in opposition to the dominant culture of the school. Though a companion study undertaken by Lambert (1976) in a girls' school found there no deviant subculture.

This 'polarization' could occur not only in overtly streamed situations, but also where attempts were made to mix ability. Attention was now directed, in the study of the evolving school system at both primary and secondary levels, to observing how in classrooms and other small groups when formal distinctions of ability were removed a hierarchy of rank ordering persisted, given by the teachers and internalized by pupils. A celebrated American experiment showed the teacher's role in this labelling process. Pupil performance was altered by arbitrarily varying teachers' expectations based upon information about the pupils' abilities, thus creating 'Pygmalion in the Classroom' (Rosenthal and Jacobsen 1968). 'Labelling' became one of many explanations for the failure of even the most progressive primaries and the most comprehensive secondaries to fulfil the impossible hopes with which they had been invested. 'No less than to "break down", in a capitalist order which builds them up and is based upon them, the divisions in society of class, sex and race' (Selbourne 1981: 115). Teachers blamed themselves for the inevitable failure of their heroically misguided efforts. They could change their labelling behaviour and thus school outcomes by increasing their awareness and changing their attitudes (cf. today's 'Racism Awareness Training'). The moral was not to lower standards of expectation but to treat each child equally with regard to its own individual needs and abilities. But at the same time the new child-centred ideology, which Plowden had raised to dominance in the primary sector, allowed a new categorizing and typification of children in terms of a theory of developmental stages through which each child could be regarded as progressing though at different rates.

Educational Priority Areas and community schools

Teachers' attitudes, however, were only one-half of the problem. If 'Educational deprivation is not mainly the effect of poverty . . .', as Plowden asserted, 'parental attitude and maternal care are more important than the level of material needs' (HMSO 1967: 369). So problems of child-rearing presented by parents were also holding back their children. This opened up a new set of problems that might be termed those of infantile regression, for if it can be shown, as the Newsons (1963: 229) had, that, using the Registrar General's categories, the parents of class 5 babies are more than twice as likely as those of classes 1 and 2 to be less than twenty-one at the birth of their first child, and that that child is less likely to be breast-fed, potty trained, etc., where can successful remediation begin, if it is possible at all? Besides, such concern was liable to be resented as an intrusion by working people who had developed cultures and practices to make their position in society bearable.

For Plowden the attempt to break into the cycle of poverty began particularly in the Educational Priority Areas. Faintly echoing Ellen Wilkinson, the report advised, 'The programme should be phased to make schools in the deprived areas as good as the best in the country' (para. 174). As Halsey later recounted, 'Harold Wilson took it into his head one Saturday afternoon in 1968 to declare a British urban crisis with £20 million to cure it. It was, I think, yet another example of ideas drifting casually across the Atlantic, soggy on arrival and of dubious utility. It gave us the community development programme' (1977: 38). The central assumption of both CDPs and EPAs, that there were only small pockets of poverty needing to be cleared up, was immediately called into question by the local authority in Birmingham. Following Plowden's criteria, it put forward 25 per cent of the city's schools for educational priority treatment, of which the DES accepted only 8 per cent. That EPAs were more than just an educational policy, but aimed to head off the urban rioting that had occurred in America, is suggested by Midwinter's advocacy of community education: '. . . if they are disadvantaged and unhappy the hope is that they may be on the way to rationalizing their dissatisfaction creatively rather than expressing it incoherently and perhaps violently' (1972: 24). Urban riots were to come later to the UK and it is doubtful that community schools played any part in postponing their arrival. Certainly the EPAs did not substantially alter the educational and life chances of their impoverished residents.

Halsey himself acknowledged their limitations at a DES-sponsored conference on 'Educational Disadvantage' in 1975.

Meanwhile the debate over streamed versus unstreamed organization within schools repeated in a similar way the previous debate over selective or non-selective schools and arrived at similar conclusions. 'As the social background of their classmates increased, the achievement of working class children increased. Middle class children on the other hand, were apparently unaffected by the social status of their class' (Barker-Lunn 1971: 19). And again, 'Briefly, the results of the investigation showed that the effects of school organisation and type of teacher lay in the pupils' emotional and social development, rather than in the sphere of formal attainment' (Ferri 1971: 13). Perhaps this latter finding accounts for the general feeling among comprehensive school teachers that the mixed-ability class related to its own tutor as the basic element of the school's organization is so socially important, though in very few schools is that class taught as an undifferentiated group, except in a few non-academic subjects. The class registered by its tutor is in fact an administrative convenience. Even where there is mixed-ability teaching of the whole group, the same ends of discrimination and selection may be achieved by means other than streaming or any of its more refined applications in setting and banding. Nash (1973) reported that even children as young as eight gave themselves positions which correlated highly with those assigned to them by their teachers and Reay (1980: 47–9), repeating the same techniques some years later in another area of England found '. . . that within unstreamed primary school classes there is a pervasive non-overt streaming according to ability and that the resultant hierarchy is perceived in essentially the same form by both teachers and children.' In any case, Barker-Lunn's latest survey of 700 junior schools found one-third of them returning to some sort of formal streaming (as reported in *The Sunday Times*, 21/11/82). This was long before Kenneth Baker's bright idea of testing at seven, eleven and fourteen promised to accelerate these competitive processes.

Whether a school which streamed, banded or set could call itself a 'true' comprehensive remained a vexed question. Benn posed but did not answer it when, once again, reviewing the progress of comprehensivization, this time throughout the 1970s, she reported: 'Selection still blocks the growth of comprehensives' (1980: 8–11). This was irrespective of the internal organization of schools, but because, nationally, non-selective schools were in competition with selective ones, both grammar and public. Because of the overall effect of such selection, 'If we want to be purists, we can say that probably only one third of the country's secondary population goes to a comprehensive school where there is no selection at all.' 'The DES', she noted, 'has never been anxious to acknowledge that there is an inherent conflict in running a comprehensive system alongside a grammar one.' And, 'At no stage has there been a planned, specially-funded, evolutionary programme of change from a selective to a comprehensive system. Instead there has been encouragement – or lack of it – for a series of local thrusts to establish comprehensive beach-heads inside what was, and still is, a selective education system.' Indeed with every change of government the move to comprehensivization slowed (in 1970), or was accelerated (1974), as signalled by their respective circulars. But by 1976 Callaghan and other Labour leaders spoke in the 'Great Debate' of the process having been completed. Therefore the period of educational expansion which the Labour Party had initiated in the 1960s was over.

For Benn the failure of comprehensive schools to open education to the working class was the failure to advance to a complete state system beyond the mixed economy of education. For others, comprehensives were not conceived radically enough. 'True' comprehensives would be community schools. 'The British reaction to the comparative failure of city schools and the stubborn persistence of class differentials in educational success has been to look to "the community" ', Marland declared (1980: 185).

Whether community is understood to mean the working class as a whole (as by Jackson 1968: 167) or, as in much common parlance, merely the black sections of it, the impetus for the community schools' lobby came from the EPAs. Midwinter, its foremost spokesperson and formerly of Liverpool EPA, defined the role of schools within their communities (here synonymous with their catchment areas) in the same way that the action-research tasks of the EPAs were set: 'One alternative to the growing decay of much of our urban life is community development in which community education has an important part to play. The grassroots participation which many see as the only possible breakthrough into the cycle of urban neglect and deprivation . . .' So that 'It is the task of community education to make the state's schools the people's schools.' His vision of how this would work in practice might not be shared by all his fellow enthusiasts for the community education (e.g. Hargreaves 1982). Midwinter foresees the local community '. . . overlooked by a horizontal stratum of officials, with the policemen, the legal representatives, the welfare and medical workers all pledged together in an interprofessional group . . .' (1973: 5, 71 & 50). For local people this omnipresent professional management of their lives would weave a bureaucratic mesh from which there could be no escape. However conceived, Rogers (1980: 135) quotes DES figures showing only 200 primary and secondary schools in England and Wales operating as community schools, less than one per cent of all maintained schools in 1978. It is ironic that the few areas where these schools exist are in fact areas where community in any traditional sense can least be said to exist.

For Midwinter, 'The community school achieves its aim when it becomes difficult to decide where the school ends and the community starts' (1973: 62). This echoes Illich's still more radical notion of 'deschooling'. Much discussed in colleges of education, its only practical outcomes were some thirty 'free schools'. Those that did not soon fold up were subsidized and later reabsorbed by the state system. There were also attempts by a few community projects to set up similarly shortlived 'learning exchanges'. Illich is easily mocked for his liberal anarchism, his consequent evasion of questions of political power and his ultimately millenarian vision. The derivation of his ideas from McLuhan and other apostles of a 'post-industrial' society is also significant. But he made many positive contributions in his wide-ranging critique. He recalled that 'The school system is a modern phenomenon, as is the childhood it produces' (1971: 27). He pointed out the confusion of schooling with education and insisted that real knowledge came from experience. He criticized education in a capitalist society for processing both knowledge and people into commodities. So that, 'Teachers more often than not obstruct such learning of subject matter as goes on in school' (ibid.: 29). Holt, in the same strain of American radicalism, had also asserted: 'To a great degree, school is a place where children learn to be stupid' (1964: 157), while Goodman was a home-grown variety of the same. So was D. H. Lawrence, also a former schoolteacher, who called for the closing of all schools to allow the flourishing of the natural and spontaneous (1956). However, deschooling met with a particular response at this time.

Deschooling the teachers

The bashing that teachers took from the deschoolers was part of the spread of radicalism from the universities into the colleges and the schools. Strikes by Inner London teachers had led to a successful campaign for much-improved pay. In 1972 two school pupils' unions were formed, the National Union of School Students and the Schools Action Union. The NUSS survived as a generally quiescent sometime adjunct of the NUS (lately somewhat invigorated by Militants without the NUS). The short-lived SAU induced hysteria in the popular press by leading as many as 10,000 on strike in one day in London for an end to canings, uniforms, detentions, etc. The radicalism that burnt itself out in pursuit of deschooling had an opposite face in a reformism that was equally idealistic: 'An attempt within the confines of education to bring about that transformation of individual consciousness which is seen as the key to social regeneration' (Sharpe 1975: 227). This rejected both traditional curricula, which were subjected to a heavily intellectualist critique by the 'new sociology of education' (e.g. Young 1971), and the recently rediscovered 'hidden curriculum'. This had been regarded as benignly establishing the conditions of learning in schools by Jackson (1971) who named it, but was now seen as deeply manipulative

Channan and Gilchrist (1974) urged a cultural revolution waged in schools by teachers to transform the conditions of society. Chris Searle was a teacher whose position in an East London church school had been saved by a pupil strike after he published a volume of their poems that the governors disapproved of. He urged teachers to '. . . overcome by a comradeship of the classroom . . . the very roles and conflict the society was making for and between us' (1975, introduction). Such idealism continues to sustain many 'committed' teachers. It is still endorsed in colleges of education by academics attempting to fire their students with enthusiasm for teaching but who, as objective observers, should know better. Madan Sarup, for instance, posits schools as potential sites of struggle for transitional change to socialism within which teachers can function as Gramscian 'organic intellectuals' (1982: 73 and note on 132).

Sarup's book on *The Politics of Multiracial Education* (1986) takes this advocacy of teachers as the vanguard of political change to such lengths that its absurdity becomes obvious. He offers 'a brief sketch of the main features of a new curriculum' in which 'all young people should learn philosophy and economics.' 'I envisage the teaching in schools of historical and dialectical materialism and of not only European but also Asian and African philosophies' (117). This is not seen in an inspirational socialist future but is seriously suggested as part of 'a concerted policy of curriculum innovation' starting now. It leaves unanswered the perennial question of who is to educate the educators. The majority of teachers, as Sarup acknowledges elsewhere, voted Conservative in the 1979 and 1983 elections and would probably have done so again in 1987 if only their salary claim had been met in full. As it was, according to a MORI poll commissioned by the *TES* (29/5/87), the majority of teachers switched to Alliance. Moreover, the minority of socialist teachers is characteristically more marked by fundamental disagreements about the nature of their socialism (let alone dialectical materialism), than by unity even on basic issues.

Searle again, who as education adviser to Sheffield Council advocated anti-imperialist rather than anti-racist teaching, considers the United States imperialist but not the other superpower, the Soviet Union. Thus he came into conflict not only with fellow teachers who disagreed, but also with Asian pupils who stood by their co-religionists in opposing the Soviet invasion of Afghanistan. With disagreements as basic as this there can be no question even of a dominant group of left teachers imposing an agreed curriculum of the type Sarup imagines. Supposing it were possible though, such a curriculum would be paid only lip-service by the majority of the teaching force, like the ILEA's directives on 'Sex, Race and Class' (1985). Further, a curriculum of even the most dialectical philosophy, imposed from above within schools, would be rejected by pupils because it would not meet with the common sense of their own received culture. Nor would it correspond to an unreconstructed capitalist social order. The changes that would be required in society to make this correspondence are so vast that they could not occur without the active involvement of the mass of the population. This involvement would itself be an education more profound than any which could possibly be imagined, let alone achieved, within the confines of schools.

Most teachers in any case take refuge from any overt political commitment in the self-concept of professionalism. This ideology is also completely spurious. Teaching has none of the criteria that define the professional status of an occupation. Teachers are not self-employed and do not charge fees. They are salaried staff without control over entry to their employment. They have no independent professional body like the Law Society or the BMA to monitor standards and limit numbers. Unlike psychiatrists, for instance, there are no institutionally controlled professional groupings divided in outlook and approach, marking differing ideological orientations. But professionalism is asserted by teachers as a means of recovering a status that has been lost. As such, it is a double-edged weapon, for the employers (and the Professional Association of Teachers that disavows strikes) declare the criterion of professionalism to be the dedication to duty that renounces industrial action. Such professional protestations to be 'non-political' are clearly here exposed as highly political actions. This applies not only in strike situations but also in the cauldron of conflicting political claims which education has become. Adding fuel to the fire, the right-wing press have mercilessly made schools one of their choice targets. 'Enemies within' the school gates include at once dopey teachers, outright subversives and permissive parents (see Murray 1986 'The Press and Ideology in Thatcher's Britain').

As well as the teachers, parents were also repeatedly blamed for the failure of working-class pupils even in reorganized schools, for example, in the government report on *Parents' Attitudes to Education*. This stated that 'Parents in the manual occupation group show signs of alienation from the school which their children attend. They provide the weakest educational support for their children . . . Their homes show least evidence of literacy . . . [And] Some of these parents' other attitudes are out of step with those of the school' (HMSO 1972: 39–40 and compare the 1985 Swann Report on black parents). Within the family, language acquisition and use, providing the basic medium of communication for education, became the focus of concern. Bernstein's work in particular, couched in the quasi-Marxist terms of 'Class, Codes and Control', awakened hopes of solving class conflict by 'large-scale State intervention in the family socialization processes of the lower classes'. For, if 'It is primarily linguistic (and not, for example, socioeconomic) differences that are blamed for social inequality', then 'Social inequality (of opportunity) can be compensated by raising the standards of speech' (Dittmar 1976: 85 and 28).

The 1975 Bullock Report was the last major government report to assert the reforming ideal of education and urge an attempt to carry through that social reform by cultural change, in this case – drawing upon the work of Bernstein – by an emphasis upon language at all levels. Set up under a Conservative government as the result of a 'reading scare' (see p. 47), Bullock reported to a Labour one, which announced that it had no extra funds to implement his recommendations. It then shelved the report without even parliamentary debate, so that Bullock himself said the government was not interested in the report and never had been. He was right, for the government was no longer interested in the ideal of reforming society through education, but now sought to reshape education to fit the changing needs of society defined as industry. It still saw the way to do this as within education itself. The existing administration was to be used to increase government control by centralizing the Inspectorate, centrally monitoring the system as a whole through the Assessment of Performance Unit and the NFER, issuing policy statements on key subject areas, so promoting the notion of a 'core curriculum' and initiating the 'Great Debate'.

This centralizing tendency was maintained even when the initiative for change came from without the education administration in the form of the Manpower Services Commission's growing influence. Centralized monitoring and control will also be strengthened by schools opting out of local education authority to rely on grant funding from the central state. The attainments of the majority of schools remaining under local administration will also be centrally accounted in the proposed tests at seven, eleven and fourteen. These 'benchmark' tests will provide a means for the centre to ensure the implementation of the national core curriculum of essential subjects to which most schools may soon be reduced. Meantime the Assessment of Performance Unit continues to monitor language, maths and science performance across the whole country, although its attempts to measure standards in other subjects have not been successful so far.

The end of reform

The failure of comprehensive reform was acknowledged in the claim that the process of reform was complete. The pessimistic consensus now emerging among the government's education advisers, including the sociologists of education, accepted the institutionalization of cultural class conflict by schools and acknowledged the limits of the period of educational expansion. 'In other words relative chances did not alter materially despite expansion' (Halsey 1972: 7–8). Murdoch and Phelps present a sharp summary of the new, realistic orthodoxy: 'Secondary schools are run by middle class people (the teachers) on behalf of other middle class people (the pupils' future employers). Consequently the underlying values and assumptions of schools are those of the middle class. . . . The majority of middle class pupils expect to enter non-manual employment and to pursue some sort of career. Consequently they accept the role of "good pupil" as a necessary dress rehearsal for their adult working life. . . . However, the situation of working class pupils is very different. They know quite well that they are being prepared for a working life at a factory bench, typewriter or shop counter, and they are not going to have a career. As a result many of them see no reason to play along with the dress rehearsal.' (1973: 59–60). To even the most radical minority of teachers too, their daily experience in schools made it more and more obvious that they were contributing to maintaining the status quo rather than in any way undermining or overthrowing it.

The incapacity of the schools to eliminate or even soften class differences was highlighted by the raising of the school-leaving age in 1972. Two years after this belated reform a government report pointed to the changing nature of the youth labour market, with the loss of 400,000 jobs held by young people in the ten years to 1971 (HMSO 1974). The report alleged that substantial numbers of leavers lacked any qualifications for the jobs that were available. Raising the leaving age would hopefully improve qualifications, but it was widely and cynically seen as a way of disguising unemployment; nevertheless welcomed, by teachers' unions for example, as fulfilling a long-held aspiration of the social democratic programme at the same time as safeguarding their members' employment. The numbers obtaining qualifications had risen with the expansion of higher education and the spread of examination criteria to more jobs, as unemployment, particularly youth unemployment, also rose. Prior to ROSLA annual DES reports indicated more than 50 per cent were staying on to take some sort of exam in any case.

Despite Crosland's belief that comprehensive schools would reduce juvenile delinquency, one consequence of the raising of the school-leaving age was a corresponding rise in the peak year for juvenile crime. This phenomenon was first observed by the Crowther Report which stated, 'The last year of compulsory education was the worst year for juvenile delinquency. The steadily rising rate of delinquency in the secondary school years declined when a boy went out to work' (quoted in Rogers 1980: 7). Wilmott (1966) saw this as one of a number of 'cycles of delinquency': 'What goes on, up to and beyond this age, is stealing from or defrauding one's employer' (143). A second cycle of 'offences mainly "associated with hooliganism and disorder" ', '. . . starts later and reaches its peak at about 17' (156). Downes (1966) also emphasized the normality and predictability of this behaviour: 'Instead of regarding the working-class delinquent as a deviant in a conformity-producing society, it is possible to regard the working-class boy as born into a pre-ordained delinquency promoting situation' (260).

In the only attempt to prove that schools actually cause juvenile delinquency, Harris (1979) examined the records of 203 boys attending five comprehensive schools in an urban police division to establish 'the school reactive pattern . . . a pattern of distribution of crime in which the incidence of crime is significantly greater during term-time than it is during the holidays. . . . This pattern would seem to confirm that the formation of delinquency groups within schools is directly related to the incidence of juvenile crime; and when the groups committing joint crimes were examined, most delinquent groups appeared to have met and had their relationships sustained at school, rather than at home' (12 and 13).

If juvenile crime now rises to a peak beyond the school-leaving age for the first time, this suggests an equation of school and unemployment as states of dependency and unemployment as prolonged adolescence. The government's determination to cut social security benefits for school leavers in order to force them to accept the training allowance for a two-year YTS may also affect the situation. The peak age for juvenile crime may then rise by another two years to what is effectively a further raising of the leaving age. If trainees are thereafter returned to the dole queue, a new cycle of crime might be expected after age nineteen, if the social factors (basically, 'settling down' with 'a steady girlfriend', suggested by both Downes and Wilmott) do not act to prevent it. Not only the incidence but also the prevalence of juvenile crime may thus be increased. For, as NACRO (1987) reports on its YTS and CP schemes, 'Having a job is the single most important factor in the resettlement of offenders and the prevention of crime. Success in getting and keeping a job will determine, more than anything else, whether or not an individual will stay clear of future trouble with the law.'

The predictable corresponding rises in peak ages for

juvenile delinquency following the raising of the school-leaving age in 1947 and 1972 operated irrespective of the form of organization of the schools. Not so truancy. The move to comprehensives increased, or coincided with an increase in, truancy overall. The National Child Development Study found that comprehensive pupils self-reported the highest rates of truancy (52 per cent). Although 'We cannot report that the greater likelihood of being regarded as a truant, or of reporting having truanted, among comprehensive pupils seriously hindered their progress, overall, relative to other pupils' (Stedman 1980: 220 and 64).

High youth unemployment might have been expected to reduce these figures but while youth over sixteen have been increasingly unemployed, there has been a rise in part-time child labour for those under sixteen (see MacLennan *et al.* 1985; also Forester 1979). Changes in family economies, with one or more of the older members out of work, make it more important to have another wage earner (even if low-paid and part-time). Other factors, such as the apparent irrelevance of schooling and qualifications to securing employment and the fact that many older pupils are not easily distinguished from their unemployed elder brothers and sisters, may also have increased figures. However, Raffe (1986b) claims to have found by comparing attendance figures in areas with different rates of unemployment that high unemployment, at least in Scotland, has reduced truancy minimally among fourth-year pupils. Possibly bunking-off for the afternoon is less attractive if Dad is sitting at home watching TV!

The feelings of pupils themselves about their education have been summarized to show: '1) Primary school children tend to enjoy school, whereas secondary school children tend to be less happy with their school experiences. 2) Both "successful" and "unsuccessful" pupils in secondary schools record dissatisfaction. It is not just a reaction of the "failures". 3) The dissatisfaction appears to be marked, and not a minor feature. Only the minority of secondary schools appear to achieve even a pass mark in the eyes of pupils' (Meighan 1981: 37). This bears upon Halsey's statement that 'The state primary schools have been stable institutions in the sense of retaining the steady loyalty of most parents' (1980: 45). This is because the aim and objective of primary education – functional literacy and numeracy – is one shared by parents, pupils and teachers alike. Whereas secondaries, increasingly without any agreed and shared aim or purpose, are not so stable and parental loyalty to them was never gained or has been lost. Their instability is growing critical because of changes in the labour market they supply.

The secondary schools are the prime site of the process of selection through examination for manual or mental labour. Manual work is not restricted to labouring with a pick and shovel. As the application of new technology strips work of any skills there may have been in making and all control there ever was over the product, manual work is increasingly defined by a lack of knowledge. This knowledge and power is, also increasingly, appropriated by managers and administrators whose labour is purely mental. In giving future manual workers a sense of their own ignorance and 'brainlessness' education is crucially implicated in the distribution of knowledge, particularly scientific knowledge, in society. As the content of education has deteriorated its duration has lengthened. As has been long apparent in America, 'The schools are a baby-sitting service during a period of collapse of the old-type family and during a time of extreme urbanisation and urban mobility' (Goodman 1962: 27), so that, 'as caretakers of children and young people', schools are now 'indispensible for family functioning, community stability, and social order in general (although they fulfil even these functions badly)' (Braverman 1974: 439). Is this to be the end result of a period of reform the aim of which was to open education to the working class?

The ground laid by the 1944 Act has been described as an 'educational settlement . . . to refer to the balance of forces in and over schooling'. 'In the post-war period, we identify four such phases: the educational settlement of 1944 and of the 1950s, with origins going back to the 1930s, and a generative moment in the war itself; the critique of this settlement, and especially of the tripartitism that developed in the late 1950s and early 1960s; the installation of educational expansion of an avowedly egalitarian kind in the 1960s; the collapse of the 1960s settlement and its associated alliance in the 1970s' (CCCS 1981: 32). Such a scheme seems just, except that, like many pronouncements by the Centre for Contemporary Cultural Studies, it can be considerably simplified.

There are in fact only three phases, beginning in 1944, 1964 and 1976 respectively. 1987, as has been suggested, may also prove to be a fourth. 1964–76 is an additional periodization that can now be marked. It closes the whole period of attempted social democratic reform aimed at a system with equal access to all. It indicates a turn of the wheel full circle to reestablish upon a new basis another tripartite system of secondary education. Like the old tripartitism, this new system of schooling attempts to correspond to the (changed) needs of the economy. The Prime Minister's 1976 Ruskin speech signalled, as Stuart Hall said, '. . . the fact that Labour's historic programme in education, which spanned the post-war period, and can be summed up under the banner of "universal provision" or "comprehensivization" had reached some sort of terminal point' (1983: 2).

The exercise in public participation presided over by Mrs Williams, following Callaghan's speech, was not just 'a smokescreen to hide the cuts', as alleged by the government's leftist critics. Rather, this tedious peripatetic precursor of the SDP's founding conference was an effort to gain public endorsement for a fundamental change in direction for education, and with it, for the whole social democratic programme of class equalization and amelioration. Characteristically, apparently increased public participation concealed actual measures of increased centralization and control. 'In this process, its relentless repetitiveness must be understood as a political tactic' (Donald 1979: 33).

The Green Paper summarizing the discussions defined the new orthodoxy: 'In addition to their responsibility for the academic curriculum, schools must prepare their pupils for the transition to adult and working life. Young people need to be equipped with a basic understanding of the functioning of our democratic political system, of the mixed economy and the industrial activities, especially manufacturing, which create our national wealth.' This responsibility was too great for schools alone: '. . . industry, the trades unions and commerce should now be involved in curriculum planning processes' (HMSO 1977: 44 and 22). Beyond some modest projects of the Schools Council, the machinery whereby 'industry and commerce' (the reference to the trades unions is merely a ritual genuflection to ensure their participation) could be involved in reshaping education was not suggested in the Great Debate. Its proposals were left to be implemented by the education service itself. Even when Shirley Williams began talking about a possible government-funded scheme offering all under-eighteens without work the alternative of education or training, it was envisaged that the scheme would be run primarily by her Ministry (the DES) together with youth agencies. The Department of Employment only won control over YOP because the Labour cabinet was narrowly persuaded that it could provide the required places quicker than the DES. But the machinery for such intervention lay already to hand in the shape of the Manpower Services Commission. Established under the Department of Employment, this administered Labour's 'temporary' employment schemes. As these measures expanded and became increasingly permanent, a new government, impatient of the effort to change education from within, used the MSC to subject education to changes from without. Characteristically in its turn, established procedures were bypassed to encourage the reemergence of a new tripartite schooling for selection to higher education, technical training and the rest. The ground upon which to effect this change, if not the means to do it, had been well laid by the terms of the Great Debate.

CHAPTER 4

The myth of 'transition'

Careers guidance for human capital

One of those facts supposedly known to every schoolchild but probably not is that the expansion of Britain's public education system was stimulated by the needs of the industrial revolution and the spur of foreign competition. German applications of science to industry before the 1914–18 war spurred the first of many attempts to catch up with the opposition. The latest of these repeatedly unsuccessful efforts is ludicrously presented by one of many advertisements in Saatchi and Saatchi's £2 million campaign for the two-year YTS. Above a photograph of two models posing as feckless youth, this proclaimed: 'Watch out Japan – here come Tracy and Spikey!'

The tripartite and the comprehensive systems also claimed to meet the latest needs of industry. Both followed what is called the human capital theory which sees (as Robbins did) the production of a trained workforce as equivalent to investment in long-lived capital goods. In 1944 the future needs of industry were supposed as the same division of labour into mental and manual (the latter divided into skilled, semi- and unskilled) that had served in the past. In 1964 education was caught up in the obsession of the time with modernity and classlessness: new schools and universities open to all would produce the white-coated technicians capable of fusing the white heat of scientific revolution with rapid social advance. The 'dead end' occupations repeatedly commented upon in government reports and social research would gradually disappear – taken over by robots perhaps. Yet human capital alone, without the other technical and scientific conditions for economic advance, could not of itself produce new factories and processes, or even jobs as it turned out. The only jobs that human capital theory could generate were for the professional staffs of education industries, especially in the Third World.

The disasters of this educational model of development in the Third World are documented in Dore's description of 'The Diploma Disease' which is rampant there (1976). Similarly Berg in the USA condemned 'the education craze' which caused qualification inflation and the spread of examination criteria to all levels of job entry. This was based upon the same human capital theory, which Berg called the economic investment model of education. On the basis of empirical research in different enterprises, including the army and civil service as well as small and large companies, he queried whether higher educational qualifications were either useful or necessary to the American economy. 'His most critical finding is that with the passage of time there has been a tendency for a larger group of persons to be in jobs that utilize less education than they have. . . . Employers are convinced that, by raising their demands, they will be more likely to recruit an ambitious, disciplined workforce that will be more productive than workers who have terminated their schooling earlier. Berg's findings fail to support employer practices and convictions . . . in certain areas workers with less education but more experience perform better and earn more' (Ginzberg 1971: xi–xii; see also Bowles and Gintis 1976).

In Britain, while industry changed in ways that had not been anticipated and without the still-sought economic miracle taking place, the gap between education and employment supposedly widened. Indeed the distance between school and work was alleged to be so great that by 1976 Callaghan, as has been seen, declared it the major brake upon the country's economic advance. In particular, the problem of transition from school to work became a central target of state policy and educational endeavour. The claims to have established the problematic status of this transition period rest with a series of studies related to the effort to establish a theory of occupational choice. Such a theory was intended to be 'operationalized' by careers consultants and psychologists. In England, as far as school leavers were concerned, these were instituted in the Juvenile Employment Bureau, renamed the Youth Employment Service in 1948, again retitled the Careers Service in 1972 and then threatened with absorption into the Manpower Services Commission (see p. 79). Its Careers Officers espoused an ideology of vocational guidance while being originally under the direction of the Ministry of Labour (later the local education authorities). So repeated studies of 'the transition process' sought to resolve the ambiguity of their position at the interface between school and work.

Transition has a comforting ring because it is by definition only temporary: "The concept of a 'transition phase" in adolescence is often employed as a palliative for society's functional problems of recruiting and integrating youth into adult worlds. If it is merely "a stage they are going through", then adults frankly need not confront the problems their behaviour raises, because, after all, "they'll grow out of it" ' (Berger 1963). The origin of the concept of a transition phase seems to lie in the recognition of the lack of traditional rites of passage in modern society to mark maturity of the type described by anthropology and history (see Mead 1944; though in some societies of the past formal education only began with the passing of childhood, for example the Ancient Minoans whose education commenced at eighteen). As Bazalgette wrote, 'The transition from childhood to adulthood . . . is a long drawn-out transition in present-day Britain, unmarked by any ritual indicating change of status or responsibility. This lack of ritual . . . has consequences for different aspects of life: the key one . . . is the act of leaving school, which becomes in the young person's mind, the ritual change over point from being a child to becoming an adult' (1978: 47).

Many of the present pronouncements on the problems of transition seem predicated in Kitchen's unsubstantiated 1944 notion of a 'cultural shock' being involved in the passage from school to work. Certainly schools have often conceived themselves as culturally distinct from the world of employment. This does not necessarily validate the idea of a culture shock for pupils leaving their rarefied, academic atmosphere to meet the realities of wage labour. It ignores the fact that it is only with the greatest difficulty that most pupils make anything more than a physical transition into secondary schools in the first instance and overestimates the cultural effects of schooling upon them. Other influences upon now prevalent assumptions seem to have diffused from developmental psychology, which can in its more fanciful moments see 'adolescent transition . . . from the relatively undifferentiated prepubertal boy or girl to the highly differentiated, reproductively potent, intellectually and critically vigorous young man or woman . . .' as '. . . a change as great as that from water insect to dragon fly' (Herford 1969: 149).

To channel and direct such transformations to the best individual benefit and collective economic advantage a theory of occupational choice was developed in America. This theory assumed a free individual choosing rationally between a number of different occupations, each offering various rewards for his personal satisfaction which his choice sought to maximize. The role of careers counsellor providing vocational guidance was to facilitate a more informed choice for the individual, matching his abilities and inclinations to the jobs on offer. The freedom of the individual to sell his labour to the highest bidder was preserved, while direction of labour was banished as totalitarian. The influence upon the individual of past traditions, the narrowing of his choice by the limited range of employment available and the economic compulsion forcing him upon the labour market were ignored. Upon this theory of economic origin was grafted a psychology of developmental stages together with a sociology of roles. For Ginzberg and his associates (1951) who originated this approach, career choice, like the assumption of social roles described by the American sociologist Talcott Parsons, coincided with the biological processes of maturational development.

British variations on the theme

In Britain Ginzberg's theory was heavily qualified in a series of articles in the *Sociological Review*. Whereas Haystead (1966) generally accepted Ginzberg's unremarkable thesis that occupational choice was a largely irreversible process developing over a long period of time, he added, 'Only when we have answered the questions about how different social structural groups make a choice when they perceive themselves to be faced by competing alternatives, can we see in what sense these courses of action could be described as "rational".' Musgrave (1967) argued that the theory should cover the whole process from first through subsequent occupational choices to comprehend influences operating on individuals from birth onwards. In fact "choice" was too strong a term for the sixth-form leavers she observed who did not make a rational assessment of their abilities nor of the opportunities available to them. Finally, Roberts (1968) tested Ginzberg's hypothesis upon a random sample of 196 fourteen to twenty-three-year-old males in a London borough to test whether 1) ambitions become consistent with occupations, 2) job satisfaction increases, and 3) occupational mobility declines as careers progress. 'None of these three hypotheses derived from the theories of Ginzberg and Super have been adequately confirmed. . . . Indeed the results of the investigation, taken in conjunction with other studies of British school-leavers suggest that amongst young people in Britain at any rate, occupational choice does not play the key role in entry into employment that Super and Ginzberg suggest.'

In fact, choice seemed an inappropriate term for the process of occupational selection as it occurred in the British context. Keil *et al.* in the same collection of articles from the *Sociological Review* (Williams 1974) discounted the assumption that any rational decisions were involved in the process at all. 'The use of the term "job entry" rather than the more usual job "choice" is intentional. The latter has connotations of rational assessment of abilities and opportunities which do not seem to be a general characteristic of those seeking work' (82). But just because entry into employment was not the result of a conscious choice, it did not mean the process was without rationality in the sense of being incapable of explanation. As another contributor to the *Review* put it: 'It is not "deviant" not to be employed, or to take up "delinquent" occupations if jobs do not exist or the achievement of reward is higher in delinquent than non-delinquent occupations. Nor is it "unrealistic" to leave school before completing the course, if continuing your education makes only a marginal difference to your occupation chances as seems to be the case for working-class youths in Britain and the U.S.' (Allen in Williams 1974: 165).

Just as more reports were indicating the influence upon school attainment of home background, it could also be shown that work aspirations were more related to home background than to potential ability. This was again the 'wastage' of working-class talent to the national economy that so exercised educational researchers. Those leaving school for un- or semi-skilled work constituted 18 per cent of the top third of the population measured in terms of mental ability (Douglas *et al.* 1968). Their choices, however, were made within a frame of reference that was narrowed to those types of employment pursued by members of their own families. As is still often the case today, many parents thought in terms of the opportunities available in their own youth, such as apprenticeship, night-school and day-release, rather than in terms of present opportunities (Lindsay 1969; cf. Ryrie and Weir 1977).

Within schools it did not escape notice that academic students received more help and career guidance, even though they needed it less, than the non-academic (Moor 1976). The 'dividing of the ways' between those remaining at school for future higher education and those leaving at the earliest opportunity lead to 'two quite different initiatory experiences [which] produce a permanent divide in the community' (Venables 1968: 4). While 'university and college students have increasingly elaborate counselling services available to them, their less sophisticated peers who are already at work and may have greater need for such intervention, have, with rare exceptions, no access to guidance' (Hill and Scharff 1976: 178). Yet despite all these facilities, last year sixth-formers maintained a marked uncertainty as to their future occupations right up to this late point in their school careers. Perhaps because for them entry into work was a less immediate prospect. Meanwhile in the universities and colleges many students rejected the whole 'bourgeois' notion of career security.

Studies of school leavers showed not only the isolation of

schools and the irrelevance of much of the careers advice that they offered, but also the failings of the (then) Youth Employment Service. Only a minority of leavers were placed in employment by the YES and many regarded it 'merely as a means of getting a job if one had not already been fixed up' (Keil *et al.* 1974: 87). Jahoda (1963) found only 15 per cent of his secondary modern last-year pupils aware of any vocational guidance function of their lecture from and interview with the Youth Employment Officer. Since, as in the Ince Report on the Service, the interview of school leaver and Officer was regarded as the lynch pin of the system, it was not very impressive that '. . . at least half the members of our sample could remember no discussion of any job other than that of their own preference.' The problem was that both sides came to the interview with different aims and needs, the leavers wanting the job of their choice and the Officer wanting to offer guidance. The interview was thus not a genuine interchange at all.

Carter similarly described the school leaver's interview. Although it was the most important contact between child and YEO, at which school and parents were also represented, 'The interview does not consist of three or four rational and disinterested beings gathered together to evaluate the evidence and deliberate upon a policy. It usually consists of people from different classes, with different norms, different ways of speaking and dressing, all playing different roles.' In this situation, 'The YEO often has a difficult job persuading children to lower their aspirations. . . . The reasons which a YEO gives to the child may not be his real reasons, but diplomatic ones; hence, the young person pours scorn on his advice . . .' (1962: 117 and 129). 'Half promises or possible opportunities are mistaken by the children as concrete offers of employment', while the YEO is trying to pin down the general choice of the child to some specific job opportunity (125). 'The enthusiast is not prepared to hear anything which detracts from his idea of what the job will be like.' At the other extreme, '. . . a chance remark by a child under pressure to state a choice may lead him to being placed in a job for which he at no time had much desire . . .' (127). So that, 'Many of the occupations which were obtained had not even entered the children's thoughts early in their last term at school' (137). Carter found a typical school suspicion of outsiders, rendering them unable to form links with local employers. While the YEO was seen as out to grab all their best pupils and push them into jobs.

Carter's account illustrates the ambiguity of the (then) YES. This ambiguity leads nearly every contributor on the subject to offer suggestions for replacing or amending the Officer's role. Whitney, for instance, proposed a youth tutor to follow up adolescents on leaving school. Similarly Keil *et al.* supported the 1961 Board of Education recommendation of one-day-a-week continuation schools for leavers. While Roberts advocated a school-based careers service. Moor in her turn recommended a 'new breed' of careers advisers, combining the virtues of careers officers with those of teachers, especially necessary as 'school leavers without jobs are in a state of limbo in which they are neither children nor working adults' (1976: 170). Scharff wanted a shamanic figure to guide the young souls through this limbo '. . . like Virgil accompanying Dante on a life journey of insight and growth' (1976: 251). While, no less fantastically, Willis (1977) called for unspecified 'interventions by revolutionaries' in the area.

Bridging the gap

A non-revolutionary intervention by the EEC Council of Ministers and the European Commission in 1976 launched a European Community Action Programme of twenty-eight projects to meet 'the educational and training needs of school leavers who find difficulty in getting or retaining suitable employment'. This was just as youth unemployment was approaching crisis levels and is an example of a practical school-to-work programme undertaken by the education authorities themselves, though funded from the EEC. As such the three 'Bridging' projects in England – in Bradford, Sheffield and London – aimed at young people either underachieving at school or facing 'problems' in their transition from school to work. In fact in Bradford it was found that 'the problems of transition' faced by young Asians were grounded in the nature of the local economy and the result of racial discrimination. In Sheffield the main problem lay with the continued absenteeism of the target group. The rapid change in the employment context in Sheffield between 1978 and 1982 led to a shift of provision from the low attainers towards trying to do something for all pupils. In London, where colleges had lost many of their former craft students while underattaining pupils were bored by conventional schooling, it had been the object of the Inspectors 'to capitalise upon the qualities and concerns of the colleges as a means of exposing the young people to a more adult and work-related environment,' as they put it in their 'Blue Book' (ILEA 1975). As employment prospects in the capital held up for some time longer than elsewhere, 'Bridging Courses' could offer an alternative route to available opportunities in the local job market for those remaining at school but not achieving the CSEs normally asked of apprentices. Soon, however, they, like the initiatives in the North, were overtaken by the chronic rise in youth unemployment and the increasingly permanent 'temporary' effort of the MSC to bridge the transition from school.

However, the experience of the ILEA's 'Bridging Courses' was incorporated in a DES conference on 'Getting Ready for Work' in 1976. This led in turn, after much interdepartmental wrangling, to Albert Booth and Shirley Williams, as the Secretaries of State for Employment and Education, announcing a pilot 'Unified Vocational Preparation' scheme to be run jointly by the DoE's Training Services Agency and the DES. The continuing lack of coordination between the two ministries contributed to delays in implementing UVP and a lack of provision for it. It would be another six years before the MSC, as the TSA became, could go ahead with a comprehensive scheme of vocational preparation, this time without the involvement of the DES.

In fact while there was work available, 'Contrary to a fairly widely accepted belief expressed in the literature, most young people did not experience severe problems of adjustment in the course of their transition from school to work', because 'For most young people there is a basic continuity in their experience at home, at school and at work' (Ashton and Field 1976: 11–12; cf. Roberts 1971: 133–4). Carter's *Home, School and Work* (1962) remains the classic account of the outcomes of education for the majority of working-class children who did not go on to experience the difficulties of further advance in the education system described by Jackson and Marsden in the same year. Carter shows aspirations shaped by the local 'climate of opinion' predominating over the limited influence of the school. Fathers might sometimes be reluctant to secure employment for their sons in the same firms they worked in themselves because of conflicts between their authority at home and at work. Yet direct influence was important to gain places especially in the most sought after, skilled manual jobs which constituted the ideal of a 'good job' for boys, the equivalent for girls being a 'nice job' in an office, where appearance could be more important than any possible influence. 'The particular occupations were not a vital matter. . . . What was important was the status which being a worker conferred' (150 and 212). This was hardly the ideal of progress through a career entertained by the school.

The gap between school and work, which only a very few found difficult to bridge, was therefore also a gap between school and home. 'To many children, the values of school had always appeared irrelevant to life as it is actually lived, but the values of work fitted in with those of the home and in the neighbourhood. Effort, enthusiasm and loyalty were advocated at school, but laughed at, or frowned upon at work. The beautiful and spiritual were insisted upon at school, whilst at work ugliness and materialism prevailed. In addition many children had got into the habit at school of only doing what they were told – no more – and were in no way shocked to find that this standard was common at work. In general, furthermore, children entered jobs in which the norms and values of the home were approximated to. . . . The "gap" was to them no more than a moderate change in routine' (210–11).

High rates of unemployment did not change and perhaps confirmed this disjunction between school values and those of home and work. 'For many youngsters in Oldfield, and others like them, anticipating careerless occupations and holding low expectations of work, any perspective which places emphasis on commitment, discipline and other work related "skills" is more than irrelevant; it actually inverts and challenges those characteristics and attitudes which sustain many working-class youngsters in wage labour. Their investment is in a marginal commitment, in ill discipline, in "messing about" and "having a laugh" which for them colour an otherwise oppressive working day' (Markall 1982: 43).

When there was work, Carter recorded an initially euphoric reaction to entry to employment. 'Young people mention especially the lack of forced discipline and the fact of earning. . . . There is a general feeling of satisfaction' (1962: 82), although this feeling may often be 'ephemeral'. Carter also found parents happy with their child's initial easy adjustment to work: 'Children no longer had the "moods" from which their parents had suffered during their last year at school. . . . Their sons and daughters were now more happy, more capable and more confident . . .' (65). Subsequently Carter described a pattern of frequent job-changing; one third of his sample changing their employment within a year of leaving school. Carter could find no single reason for this job-changing, except for a general dissatisfaction with what was, in the main, boring and repetitive work There was also a tendency to drop out of apprenticeships with their demanding courses of study and into dead-end jobs without further prospects. 'They did not care where they went or what they did. One job was as good, or bad, or, to all intents and purposes, the same as the next' (213).

Employers anticipated this high turn-over of juvenile labour; consequently provision for young workers came low on their list of priorities. From these frequent subsequent changes, even more than in the vagaries of the initial transition, Carter concluded that the job pattern depended '. . . as much, if not more, upon fortuity and aimless or uninformed drifting as upon intention and design' (194). This established pattern of frequent job-changing interspersed with periods of unemployment is one reason that the gradual increase in youth unemployment throughout the 1970s to the 'crisis' levels at the end of the decade caused no immediate disruption of traditional expectations. Periods between different casual and deskilled employments just grew longer for an increasingly large minority that eventually became the majority. With the advent of YOP and YTS, chronic scheme-changing replaced frequent job-changing.

Studies of adolescence presented the same general picture of work adaptation. Wilmott, for instance, tracing the different 'cycles of delinquency' which he distinguished among 'Adolescent Boys in East London', found a falling off from the peak in the last year at school which he associated with a 'honeymoon' phase when first at work. 'Later the job is likely to pall and excitement about "independence" gives way to resentment at adult authority. But as the boys mature they apparently become more content with their lot' (1966: 119). Wilmott speculated whether this was because the boys were accorded adult status by their workmates or because it coincided with 'settling down' into courtship and marriage. In between these two stages the most 'discontented' age was seventeen and eighteen, when 'They care less than formerly what their parents think, but they have not yet acquired a girl friend whose opinion of them matters. When they do acquire one and move towards a family of their own, they become once again more subject to the social controls of the local community and the national society' (162). Job-changing then ceases and they have to 'like it or lump it' with increasing responsibilities. In careers consultants' jargon, they achieve 'vocational maturity', the end point in the developmental process of the individual psyche.

'*Industrial Sociology*' also accepted an unstable and dislocated pattern of employment as normal for young workers, a pattern of job-changing or sampling that declined in volume towards the end of adolescence (Miller and Form 1964). As a young informant put it many years later: 'They change jobs very quickly; have periods of temporary unemployment; get another job; can't stand it and leave. . . . It all ends when you get married, then you have to keep the job you're in, hate it or not' (Corrigan 1979: 92).

This sort of employment was described in a DES pamphlet: 'Jobs which require no particular educational qualification and for which at present no training is necessary . . . There seem to be a great number of such jobs which are very much alike in that they require little or no academic ability and can be done by almost anyone, an impression strengthened by the knowledge that many adults switch from one job to another without any difficulty' (HMSO 1965: 42–3). Matthews (1963) claimed that 79 per cent of his sample of educationally subnormal boys could be placed in normal employment since it required only a mental and emotional age of twelve. This claim was repeated in the first official report on youth unemployment: 'We have heard it said that Careers Officers find it easier to help pupils from ESN schools because they came out better equipped to face the world and tackle a job of work than pupils from the lower streams of comprehensive and modern schools' (HMSO 1974: 37). Given the whole tone of that report (see p. 83), this was doubtless intended as an indication of pupils' attitudes as encouraged by their schooling, but it is surely more revealing as a comment upon the types of jobs themselves.

As unemployment rose, Moor (1976) found the informal connections of what she called 'the recruitment network' assuming even greater importance and leading to a further loss of respect for the careers institutions of school and state. These could only help pupils wanting jobs that required qualifications for which further study was necessary. Those who wanted to work immediately were not necessarily short-sighted however. For '. . . it is not only those from middle-class backgrounds who have long-term goals, as some research in the past has implied' (72). Ashton and Field also noted '. . . the inability of the existing body of knowledge to account for the eagerness and obvious pleasure with which some young people enter what are often referred to as "dead end" jobs . . .' (1976: 12). Willis found it 'astonishing' and his book attempted to present the 'moment – and it only needs to be this for the gates to shut on the future – in working class culture when the manual giving of labour power represents both a freedom, election and transcendence, and a precise insertion into a system of exploitation and oppression for working class people' (1977: 120). His small bunch of 'lads' were not astonished; they knew that they were not among that minority of 'arseholes' who pass exams and that if they were then someone else would not be. Willis romanticized their attitude and his study was severely restricted both in numbers and in vision. It ignored the majority of average pupils between the two poles of the 'lads' who rejected school and the 'arseholes' who accepted its values. These poles correspond to the top twenty and bottom forty divisions respectively.

In fact it is the situation of the middle forty that is increasingly critical. Their compliance with school norms is only sustained by an adherence to a culture of working-class respectability by which they differentiate themselves from middle-class 'swots' above and the 'rough' lads (and lasses) below. This self-identification is steadily undermined by the disappearance of 'good' jobs represented by apprenticeships for boys and office jobs for girls. Like traditional gender identifications, the cultural desire to be 'normal' or 'ordinary' (in the kids' own words) still survives after the labour market conditions that sustained it have altered beyond recognition. Nowadays the survival of these orientations depends more upon wishful thinking than any realistic assessment of the actual situation.

Despite its limitations, when it appeared Willis's *Learning to Labour* was important because for the first time the previously separated concerns of schooling and transition to work were integrated. It is ironic that, just when the two strands of studies of what happened to pupils within schools and what happened to them when they left were at last brought together, a new state agency was created precisely to deal with the labour problems arising from widening unemployment. The Manpower Services Commission appropriated the accepted notions of 'transition' from school to work as a rite of passage. It represented the need for an institutional 'bridge' between the two supposedly culturally distinct 'worlds of school and work'. It also popularized ideas of more 'relevant' and less academic schooling to erode this separation. It then effected a sea-change in their use. What had seemed previously the terms of a progressive critique of existing education became justifications for a new economic rationalization. School culture, on one side, was accepted as an influence from which the young had to be institutionally desocialized. The world of work, on the other, was presented as the unproblematic and natural arena in which individuals find their self-fulfilment and achieve 'vocational maturity'.

The existing arrangement for guiding this 'transition

process', that provided by the Careers Service, had been shown by all the transition studies reviewed above to occupy an ambiguous position between the 'two worlds'. Under the MSC it was preserved and given a new role. Especially with the introduction of the Youth Training Scheme as 'a permanent bridge between school and work', the Careers Service has remained the major referral agency for young people onto schemes. Indeed at the launch of YTS in the autumn of 1983, a Minister from the Department of Employment warned the annual conference of the Institute of Careers Officers that their service was on trial and its future depended upon how it handled the new scheme. Put simply, without careers to guide people into there is little point in running a careers service which costs the annual equivalent of the Civil List. This is hardly a politic admission to make, however, and although the goverment was attempting to reduce the Civil Service, the absorption of 3,500 Officers plus support staff presented problems. So for a time the Careers Service's ambiguous role was sustained. Throughout the first years of YTS the MSC used the Careers Service to advise and inform about the Scheme in schools and under local government authority where it might be difficult for the Commission itself to intervene directly.

CHAPTER 5

The failure of vocationalism (1976–1987)

The ministry of training

The Manpower Services Commission or Training Commission as it was renamed in April 1988, has come to command the position of a de facto Ministry of Training with inordinate influence over post-sixteen education. Through its inroads into further education, the youth service and adult education and training, it also has direct (through TVEI and teacher training) and indirect influence upon secondary education. As has been argued, the 'Great Debate' finally closed the period of educational expansion. The Debate also officially endorsed a recognition of the failure of that expansion to achieve the social objectives set for it by social democracy. This failure was rationalized in economic terms. Education was blamed for the lack of trained manpower imbued with the necessary attitudes to work. This was supposedly causing the crisis manifested in the rise of (particularly) youth unemployment. Blaming education for the failings of the economy may seem ridiculous but was merely the obverse of Labour's previous enthusiasm for solving economic problems through educational reform. The Debate still proposed to effect the required changes through the existing educational channels. These efforts continued through the traditional means of increasingly centralized ministerial direction and control. However, the MSC, as the most effective instrument of change, had long lain to hand outside of and unhampered by the traditional pressures upon the educational bureaucracy and its local accountability.

Much journalistic copy but no authoritative historical study has recorded 'the rise and rise of the MSC', as the *Guardian* (10/11/77) called it (but see Ainley and Corney forthcoming). From its establishment by the 1973 Employment and Training Act with a secretariat of forty, numbers of staff peaked at 26,162 in 1979. Costs mounted to over £2,000 million for 1984–5 (compared with the £1,300 million Exchequer grant to all UK universities for that year). £3 billion was forecast for the MSC's 1987–8 budget. Suffice to say here that the MSC was carved out of and influenced by the Department of Employment. It took over management of the Industrial Training Boards, Job centres and TOPs courses then funded at £15 million a year. This sort of 'hiving off' to independently managed agencies of government departments had been proposed by the Fulton Committee. It was hoped that the specific policy objectives of such organizations would be more easily attained than in Whitehall departments preoccupied with a range of issues and responsibilities. The 1972 consultative document 'Training for the Future' suggested a national training agency along Swedish and West German lines. Like them, the new body embraced in its ten-man Commission industry and the unions, plus local authority and an education representative. (The only woman commissioner represented the CBI for a year until January 1985.) MSC is not, however, tripartite in the strict sense, being without government representation though under the 'direction' of the Secretary of State for Employment. With the Labour government conciliating the unions in exchange for wage restraint, 'Among the less controversial and seemingly less costly proposals of the TUC was the establishment of a Manpower Commission – an idea which reflected the influence of European models on TUC officials and which was also acceptable to officials in the Department of Employment. In this way the commission was superimposed on existing services already moving towards semi-independent status . . .' (Howells 1980).

Significantly, the establishment of the MSC merged two policy areas – those designed to combat unemployment and training policies. As Moon and Richardson wrote, 'Training policies have not simply been used as a means of preparing members of the workforce for new jobs, but also as a means of removing large numbers of people from the unemployment register. This merger has been most obvious in the case of schemes for youth' (1985: 73). Initially the MSC was divided into two bodies each with its own organizational structure: the Employment Services Agency and the smaller Training Services Agency. Their autonomy was reduced by reorganization in 1978 when the MSC acquired a corporate identity in its new headquarters in Sheffield. This enabled it to act in a more concerted fashion. Training Services were merged in 1982 with the Special Programmes Division to form a new Training Division, preparing for the operation of YTS with a local network of Area Manpower Boards.

Three reports prepared the ground for the new commission. *Unqualified, Untrained and Unemployed* (HMSO 1974) outlined the scope of the problem. The number of jobs held by young people had fallen by 400,000 between 1961 and 1971. Employers preferred 'steady' adults and women with children returning to work part-time to young people given to frequent job-changing and with 'irresponsible' attitudes. For 'a large minority of unemployed young people seem to have attitudes which, whatever their cause or justification, are not acceptable to employers and act as a hindrance to young people in securing jobs' (29). Attitudes were what counted, not examination success. The report rehearsed the literature to show that substantial numbers of apprentices lacked any qualification. Thus, there was 'no reason why an unqualified boy or girl with the right personal qualities should not aspire to an apprenticeship or a clerical job in regions where these jobs are available' (22).

Following the TSA's Five Year Plan in 1973, Chris Hayes's *Vocational Preparation for Young People* (TSA 1975) designated young entrants to the workforce as a 'priority group of special national importance'. It noted the demands from industry upon these new workers for generalized and flexible abilities rather than the former apprenticeships in particular skills. 'A more responsible attitude' was again required for this adaptation. It was in their failure to cultivate this attitude that schools were identified as failing the national economy. 'In recent years the social environment of a number of schools, with more emphasis on personal development and less on formal instruction, has been diverging from that still encountered in most work situations. There the need to achieve results in conformity with defined standards and to do so within fixed time limits calls for different patterns of behaviour. The contrast is more marked where changes in industrial processes have reduced the scope for individual action and initiative' (15).

Employers also increasingly vented the same opinion, partly in order to fend off the TSA's proposals for 'Gateway' training which they regarded as outside their responsibility and superfluous to their needs. Arnold Weinstock, under the headline 'I blame the teachers' (*TES* 23/1/76), declared: 'Employers are firmly of the view that shortcomings in the vocational preparation of young people are basically an educational problem which cannot be passed on to the employers under the guise of training and induction.' Since the schools were alleged to have caused the problem and employers were unwilling to pay for its remediation, the correction of irresponsible attitudes hampering increased adaptability and flexibility would fall to a new state agency. Holland (later MSC Director) saw this in his 1977 *Young People and Work* (TSA: 1977), which followed the TSA's Review for 1975 in recognizing that full employment had 'not been interrupted but ended' (8). Youth unemployment was thus no longer a temporary problem but a permanent feature demanding new and equally permanent measures to contain it.

What this presentation of the problem could not obscure was the fact that 'changes in industrial processes have reduced the scope for individual action and initiative'. These changes altered the nature of the workforce that was now required. In particular, automation with its consequent deskilling was undermining the traditional distinctions between un-, semi- and skilled manual labour. 'Although it is impossible to define these categories with any degree of precision, the terms are commonly used and understood throughout industry. It is generally accepted that a skilled worker is a craftsman whose training has been spread over several years and is formally recognized outside an individual firm; a semi-skilled worker is one who, during a limited period of training, usually between two and twelve weeks, has acquired the manual dexterity or mechanical knowledge needed for his immediate job, and an unskilled worker is one whose job requires no formal training of any kind' (Woodward 1965: 28–9). The arbitrariness of such divisions is clear. In fact, the division between un- and semi-skilled is one not based upon the nature of the task but imposed upon it for the convenience of management. There has been an increasing tendency for jobs previously described as 'casual' to be redesignated 'semi-skilled' by adding 'training programmes' as a form of work discipline. Corresponding with this there has been a consequent shift in recruitment from school leavers to those aged twenty-two and above. Such redesignations are notorious as ways for employers to circumvent the provisions of, for example, equal opportunities legislation. Further, they can operate quite arbitrarily up or down the labour hierarchy independently of the actual amount of skill required of the worker. This has always been to the disadvantage of the least experienced and reliable youth. 'Previously, many of the unskilled and unqualified young have found work in casual trades where their control depended on direct discipline and supervision – such jobs are now being reorganized. As industry reduces its workforce, there is less spare labour power to provide either on the job training or continuous supervision. Firms find it cheaper and more "rational" to recount workers who do not need such training and supervision, who are already relatively self-disciplined and reliable. Casual labour is transformed into "semi-skilled work" ' (Finn 1984: 82). The decline of apprenticeships further blurred the old craft distinctions. As new technology stripped craftsmanship of its slowly acquired skills, skilled work was also transformed into semi-skilled.

The MSC recognizes this transformation of the workforce with its calls for 'flexibility' and 'adaptability' increasingly required of an undifferentiated and semi-skilled mass. But responsibility for the desired change in attitudes was not laid with industry that had made the change necessary. Rather, education was blamed for not cultivating the newly demanded mentality. The MSC could not at first offer its own solution to the problem of wrong attitudes. It was immediately preoccupied with the perceived threat to public order presented by rising numbers of unemployed youth. The first of its various temporary schemes to meet the crisis was the Job Creation Programme. As part of the bargain struck by the government with the TUC in the Social Contract, JCP provided 100,000 temporary jobs during 1975–77. Lindley (1980) has compiled a splendid list of acronyms for all these emergency efforts of the Special Programmes Division: 'Temporary Employment Subsidy (TES) – Temporary Short-Time Working Compensation Scheme (TSTWCS) – Small Firms' Employment Subsidy (SFES) – Recruitment Subsidy for School Leavers (RSSL) – Youth Employment Subsidy (YES) – Adult Employment Subsidy (AES) – Job Creation Programme (JCP) – Special Temporary Employment Programme (STEP) – Work Experience Programme (WEP) – Community Industry (CI) – TSA Course for Young People (TSAYP) – Youth Opportunities Programme (YOP) – Training Places in Industry (TPI) – Job Induction Scheme for Disabled (JIS) – Job Release Scheme (JRS)' (345). There have been many more since.

From YOP to Son of YOP

YOP also began by fulfilling the government's side of the bargain with the TUC leadership. It provided what was seen as a short-term response to the hopefully temporary and cyclical phenomenon of mass youth unemployment. The work preparation and prevocational training it offered led 80 per cent of its first 162,000 graduates (1 in 8 of all school leavers) to find employment or further training. The allowance paid them was equivalent to £40 at prices current with the later YTS allowance of £27.50. However, as the numbers on the scheme rose to half a million by 1981/2, its placement rate fell below 25 per cent together with a fall in the quality of any training provided. A report by Youthaid (1984), commissioned and financed but not published by the MSC, on the experiences of West Midlands school leavers on YOP could, as the authors say, equally well be applied to the YTS: results of the programme were that the numbers of young people in skilled jobs fell sharply; they suffered an 18 per cent fall in living standards; YOP failed to increase their skills and condemned most of those lucky enough to get jobs to unskilled work, low pay and bad working conditions. Loney, writing a 'Requiem' for the Programme and foreseeing its 'Rebirth' in YTS, concluded that 'many programmes are so badly organised . . . [they] succeeded, not in introducing young people to the world of work, but rather to a world of constant confusion' (1983: 28).

Whilst criticism of YOP as an unsafe, cheap-labour scheme rose from trade unionists and young people themselves, the government continued to support the programme. It thus appeared to do something about unemployment at the same time as cutting the funding for further education, the ITBs and the MSC's other programmes. In 1980 the EEC commissioners who provided from the Social Fund £48 million of the £144 million estimated cost of YOP refused to grant an additional £30 million requested on the grounds that the money was not for additional training but only provided temporary employment. This YOP had always been, but YTS presented itself as something radically different. Yet five years later the EEC again withdrew its £70 million contribution to YTS on the grounds that the scheme did not involve young people in new technology training.

The idea of a vocational preparation scheme for all young people had first been suggested by the TSA in 1974. However, a permanent youth training scheme was only forced upon the agenda by the 1981 urban riots or 'Uprisings'. This was exactly the response to mass youth unemployment that the series of temporary employment measures had been designed to avoid. There was also until then a reluctance to admit to the permanence of such high levels of unemployment, a clinging to the post-war commitment to full employment. The new realism of monetarism now established a new consensus. 'The days of "full employment" are not only over; they are as much a part of social history, which we may regard with nostalgia or contempt according to taste, as hoolahoops and spats' (Sinfield 1981: 1). So the change of government also marked a turning point: 'On the one hand, the very existence of the MSC was confirmed along with its major programmes; on the other, its period of almost uninterrupted growth was clearly at an end' (Howells 1980: 305). In June 1979 the Department of Employment announced substantial cuts in MSC spending.

This soon changed when, following the riots, YTS

presented itself as radically different from any of its temporary predecessors. It was to be both permanent and universal (supposedly for every sixteen-year-old school leaver – employed and unemployed alike). It is, however, directly continuous with the discredited YOP. Both promised places to every unemployed school leaver. Both offer training for increasingly deskilled occupations. Both pay an allowance only slightly better than supplementary benefit as a means of reducing youth wages and through them all wages. Although the element of compulsion was, for a time, narrowly avoided as the price of continuing TUC cooperation with the MSC, repeated threats continued to be made. Leaks from think-tanks and Prime Ministerial interviews, as well as efforts to lean on Careers Officers and the DHSS, promised benefit reductions to youngsters refusing a place. The self-styled 'Minister for Training' Peter Morrison, for example, instructed Chief Education Officers and their staffs to inform DHSS about YTS refusers in 1985. Already in 1984/5 11,000 youngsters had their benefit cut for leaving Schemes and 2,000 for refusing to join them. However, the threat of compulsion is also not a new one: Callaghan's Employment Secretary, the 'left-wing' Albert Booth, also wanted to deny the dole to youngsters who refused to join YOP. The incomplete take-up of the Scheme (one in three places reported empty in *The Guardian* 14/2/85), can only be reduced by such cuts in or abolition of benefit. The 1985 budget again promised that 'unemployment will no longer be an option' for young people by 1986. Eventually this commitment was written into the 1987 Conservative manifesto for implementation that year.

Both YOP and YTS, far from alleviating unemployment, actually aggravate it by displacing employed workers with young temporary trainees. The MSC eventually conceded that one in three places created on YOP cost the job of a permanent worker. As Loney remarked, 'It is characteristic of the MSC's performance that it took three years to discover that employers had been taking advantage of the scheme to reduce permanent staff and replace them with YOP-funded trainees. Those in the field saw this happen in 1978' (1983: 28). Without this job substitution neither scheme could work. This is acknowledged in government reports on the

Scheme, such as that of the Auditor General (HMSO 1985c). Apart from its concern with MSC's inadequate accounting procedures and its waste of at least £55 million on filled places, this states, 'YTS may have initially assisted the continuing decline in the number of permanent, employed training places in manufacturing industries' (para. 3.13). 'Additionality', by which the government pays employers to replace two young workers with five trainees, endorses job substitution. It also ensures a degrading competition between the five trainees for the two jobs that may be available at the end of the year. By subsidizing employers who give young people menial tasks and then return them to the dole queue, YOP/YTS increase employers' reliance upon state monies to employ temporary trainees whom they do not have to train. The Young Workers' Scheme also subsidized cheap labour by paying £15 to employers who paid below £45 per week. Hardly the 'real jobs' that the government said it was bent upon creating. There has also been flagrant abuse of the YWS by employers paying young workers much less than the national minimum wage, which the Department of Employment was responsible for enforcing, while still receiving subsidies for doing so. Meanwhile apprenticeship training, which was offered under the ITBs, has been all but eliminated in the name of ending 'restrictive practices' and 'time serving'. One of Tebbit's first acts as Employment Minister was to scrap sixteen out of the twenty-three Industrial Training Boards and the rest passed into industrial archaeology in 1985.

In a recession employers are more than ever reluctant to spend money on training. It is cheaper to poach skilled employees from rival firms. Despite the cheap labour that it offers them though, many employers prefer to continue with traditional methods of recruitment rather than become involved in the YTS. This is especially the case for the small businesses that together make up the majority of employers. Nevertheless, most YTS placements are in small, non-unionized, low-paying workplaces, the same small shops and businesses that were involved in YOP. The first major survey of employers' relation to YTS found: 'The most important advantage to employers participating in the YTS is the opportunity it gives them to look at or screen young people before offering permanent employment. Also very important are the "savings that result on labour costs",' Sako and Dore, reported under the title 'How the YTS Helps Employers'. Yet selling the Scheme to employers is one of the major problems facing MSC upon which the whole future of YTS hinges, particularly its radical attempts to impose unified training standards to agreed specifications through the National Vocational Qualification Framework (see page 111). The 1985 budget optimistically assumed employers would pay for YTS's second year. This was abandoned by the time the two-year Scheme started in 1986. Similarly, it was suggested that employers would be the benefactors for an expanded TVEI covering selected schools in all local authorities. However, employers are extremely reluctant to make investments without guaranteed returns, let alone donate large sums to training of doubtful utility. They were also noticeably loath to fund Mr Baker's planned City Technology Colleges.

YTS gave incentives to a new brand of small entrepreneur, the private managing agents. These were entrusted with much of the Scheme's delivery. They have been much criticized (see Birmingham Trades Council 1984; also numerous issues of *Private Eye*) for the specious claims of their advertising, the poor quality of their training and the shoddy way in which their schemes were cobbled together in exchange for the £1,950 grant MSC initially gave them for every Trainee. When the anticipated numbers on YTS did not, such was consumer resistance, approach the profitable, it was widely felt to be only just that many of these agencies became bankrupt. But the precedent they established for the future privatizing of educational provision as a whole remains significant. The extensive training empires built up by successful agencies, like Community Task Force, now make them indispensable for administering the YTS.

Hierarchies of disadvantage and discrimination

A hierarchy of both YOP and YTS quickly developed. Despite the common elements all Schemes are supposed to share, YTS is not so much a unified system as a collection of different schemes with the few Information Technology

Centres at the top and the old Mode B2s for the disabled and the disadvantaged at the bottom. This was also continuous with the past, when '. . . some of the most attractive (to employers) of unemployed youngsters had found MSC-sponsored placement with local employers (WEEP schemes) whereas the "least able" formed a residual group with only the limited facilities of the Community Service Agency available to them. Such stratification was never the intention of the programme but was nevertheless discovered to be its effect in practice' (Finn and Markall 1981: 65). YTS was designed and marketed as a one-year foundation for employed and unemployed alike. 'It is first and last a training scheme' (TSA 1981: 9) and 'not about youth unemployment' ('Youth Task Group Report', MSC: 1982, 1). Soon, however, YTS came to be used by many managing agents as a scheme only for the unemployed, just like YOP. In its first year the number of employed trainees anticipated was revised downwards from 33 per cent to only 5 per cent. Now the two-year Scheme guarantees a place only to the unemployed. The nature of this much-vaunted 'Christmas guarantee' is more that of an offer that cannot be refused.

In some regions it could be said that 'Round here the black kids go on YOPs and the white kids get jobs' (Tower Hamlets Trades Council 1981: 27). A 1984 CRE report on YTS found fewer black youngsters on courses likely to lead to permanent employment and a study for the MSC surveying three different areas also found black youngsters less likely to be on Mode A employer-based schemes and more likely to be on Mode B schemes (MSC 1984b). This was born out by a survey reported in the Transport and General Workers Union's YTS Bulletin (issue 12, 6/87) that found 100 company-based schemes in Manchester with no black trainees at all, while nearly half of black trainees were concentrated in six out of nearly 300 schemes. Similarly West Midlands County Council reported evidence of 'systematic discrimination' in the local training schemes run by the MSC (1986). Such is the accumulated evidence already that it can be safely asserted: 'The Youth Training Scheme, rather than providing a means for ethnic minority school leavers to overcome their disadvantaged position in the labour market, is in fact perpetuating and reinforcing existing inequalities'

(Austen 1984: 68). What Pollert called 'the patronizing "special needs" approach' functions to connect ethnic minorities with vocational preparation programmes but not with skill training, new technology or professional jobs (1986).

Young women on both YOP and YTS continue to be overrepresented in schemes involving traditionally low-paid feminine work. In 1984 64 per cent of girls on YTS were in administrative/clerical or sales/personal service work (*Report on YTS Leavers Survey*, MSC 10/84) while less than 3 per cent of trainees at the Information and Technology Centres were female. Meanwhile, young men continue to follow traditional gender divisions of labour unchallenged on the majority of schemes. 'Despite fine words from the MSC on equal opportunities, the evidence suggests that the YTS will not confront racism and sexism, but will institutionalize divisions within the labour force and perpetuate inequalities' (Scofield *et al.* 1983: 19). Since the MSC monitoring of its equal opportunities policy consisted of a two-person unit staffed usually by men, there could be little confidence that this prophecy would not be fulfilled. Rather, YTS reflects and reinforces the existing segregation of the labour market, following traditional practice and employers' expectations (see *Women and YTS: A report*, NUS Women's Unit 1985). MSC programmes for the young (male) unemployed soak up such semi-skilled work as is available and so marginalize still further married women characteristically forced to reenter the labour market at a lower level than they left it. Ideologically the government encourages women to remain at home, while practically the MSC does not attempt to retrain them.

In Scotland YTS has been divided by Raffe (1986a) into a typology of four sectors that would seem to apply elsewhere. At the top of the pile are those schemes guaranteeing employment in large companies to trainees subject only to their attaining minimum levels of performance. These are mainly apprenticeships brought within the Scheme. They are highly selective, make up 18 per cent of all Mode A trainees, are paid an average wage of £41, enjoy better training on the job plus an average thirty-two weeks instruction off it and are classified as apprentices or long-term trainees in the MSC's

1984 survey of managing agents (*YTS Providers' Survey*, Youth Training Board 1985).

Next come schemes offering training if not jobs in occupationally specific skills that are in demand in the local labour market. These skills are certified by the colleges or other agents running them in ways that are credible to future employers. They do not guarantee access to work but they offer a pretty good chance.

Thirdly, other schemes offer no certainty of acquiring skills nor of gaining employment. Mostly small employers use them to screen potential recruits should vacancies arise. Therefore there is at least some chance of employment. 'Employers who use YTS to screen for permanent employment may also be relatively selective when taking on young people for the YTS year, though nationally the majority of YTS schemes do not have formal entry requirements' (Sako and Dore 1986). On schemes in larger companies offering some chance of employment through this preselection process, 'the catchment areas for recruitment were typically in the suburbs. Others had introduced recruitment criteria such as four O levels' (Davies and Mason 1986: 18); while a well-known West End firm advertised, 'Having successfully completed two years under the YTS, should you wish to be employed by the company and complete a third year's training, there will be a training fee of approximately £300'!

Lastly, there are the Mode B (now redesignated 'Premium') schemes, run mostly by private managing agents, completely detached from the processes of selection and recruitment of labour. As well as the old Mode Bs, these include 'Mode A schemes set up largely as an expression of social responsibility by the employers . . . where the additional "goats" are from the start distinguished from the "sheep" who comprise the normal intake' (Raffe 1986a: 20).

This hierarchy closely relates to the hierarchy within education and to the employment prospects of trainees. Since it is these which determine allocation to the different types of scheme, 'The major occupational selection will continue to be made at 16 rather than 17 or 18' (ibid.). The longer duration of YTS only accentuates this differentiation within the scheme. The role of the old Mode A, employer-based schemes is enhanced. In areas without such large employers YTS is restricted to work experience in small firms and Premium places only. While the erasure of modes 'to eradicate the false perception of first and second class trainees within the scheme' (MSC 1985: 9) cannot hide the gap between those for whom YTS offers a route into employment and those on Premium/Mode Bs for whom it does not. So the training initiative, which entertained the dual function of training and occupying the unemployed simultaneously, will increasingly split into its two separate parts: one actually training for real jobs (or further qualifications for available jobs) and the other offering occupational therapy for surplus labour. Between these two, small employers may continue to use the scheme to gain cheap labour and compliant employees as and when they require them.

Assembling the lightboxes

The new training initiative represents an attempt at a major modification of the transition from school in which the state increasingly forecloses upon young people's options. This is part of an attempted restructuring of the entire workforce, beginning with the youngest entrants to it, to meet the latest demands of recapitalization. The dependence of youth upon their families and upon state agencies is being extended. As long ago as 1976 the TSA suggested reducing the supply of labour by making sixteen to nineteen a 'Learning Period' for all young people. While Geoffrey Holland in an interview with *Personnel Management* (12/81), indicated that 'If we are to move forward, we might have to look at keeping young people in some way out of the labour market until they are eighteen.' Although certain individual civil servants and groups of politicians and their advisers have long seen this approach as a way forward for themselves and their ideas, the policy lacks the coherence that is attributed to it, for instance, by Bernard Davies (1986). His book *Threatening Youth* sees a coherent effort by all sectors of the state dealing with young people to create a new national youth policy. This policy at once constructs youth as threatening to the state and so aims to contain them. Thus it is at the same time threatening to them. Rather than such a conspiratorial collusion between different state agencies, however, there has in fact been a consistent ad hoc response to the unanticipated crisis of youth unemployment and industrial restructuring. Just because the policies were made up as they went along though, does not mean the end result cannot be welded together into the consistent form that has an appearance which Davies attributes to deliberate design. It does mean that the structure is riven by profound contradictions.

Prolongation of social childhood by YTS contradicts another aim of the new training initiative which is to maintain labour discipline in the absence of work. MSC's former Chairman, Sir Richard O'Brien, was quite explicit about MSC's role in preventing the unemployed young becoming the 'enemies of society' (Josiah Mason lecture, Birmingham University, 29/11/77). The insistence on schemes of work-analogous hours of attendance to which allowances are directly tied clearly shows this attempt to provide a substitute for work. In earlier days 'the able bodied poor were set to work though in more recent years this phrase has been replaced by the euphemism of training' (Swann and Turnbull 1978: 162). Sheldrake and Vickerstaff also note the reemergence of what they call this 'poor law effect' in their excellent though brief 1987 *History of Industrial Training in Britain*. Peter Morrison revealed his idea of the YTS in a Commons debate in July, 1983: 'the scheme is not a social service. Its purpose is to teach youngsters what the real world of work is all about. That means arriving on time, giving of their best during the working day, and perhaps staying on a little longer to complete an unfinished task.'

At its most extreme this was embodied in the Coventry lightbox assembly established by MSC and described by its supposedly more liberal and enlightened collaborator the Further Education Unit as follows: 'Here trainees construct, wire and test equipment, then package it and write the accompanying advice notes. The organisation is tight and efficient, and a convincing assembly regime is produced. When the lightboxes reach their destination in the main College building they are dismantled and their components fed back for reassembly' (FEU 1978). That this extraordinary modern version of digging holes and filling them in again took place in something calling itself a College shows to what extent education has given way to training for labour discipline. Indeed, general discussions of the purpose of work and other 'political' topics have been ruled by the MSC as beyond the scope of social and life skills classes for trainees.

Government similarly and repeatedly attempts to rule any fundamental discussion of YTS off the agenda of public debate. Mrs Thatcher dismissed the 'professional moaners' who criticized her policies. At the same Conservative Party conference Lord Young stated that there was only one thing that made him see red – 'the left-wing wreckers in our society who run down the YTS'. Bryan Nicholson told teachers on an in-service training course that teachers who opposed YTS were 'a major threat to the scheme' (*TES* 17/1/86). Elsewhere he declared that the two-year YTS 'will silence all but our most intransigent critics', who were 'knockers . . . out to sabotage the scheme' and thus Britain's economic recovery. In fact these few 'enemies within' have been submerged beneath a deluge of publicity selling the scheme with £3 million advertising campaigns from Saatchi and Saatchi, as well as the numerous MSC press releases relayed dutifully by an obliging media. (When John Pilger reported unfavourably for the *Daily Mirror* on the YTS, then-employment Minister Tom King was given an inserted box to correct the 'misleading argument' of the article, 2/85.)

Few of the MSC's critics really have much heart in their opposition to the YTS anyway. Many potential critics (researchers, lecturers, teachers, community workers, etc.) are caught up in the MSC's machinery of administration. Their present prospects and future careers depend upon MSC money. Those few who are able to operate independently can be generally relied upon to come up with the perennial researchers' conclusion that 'further research is necessary' before any definite judgement can be made. Neither they nor any of the opposition political parties have any real alternative to the scheme. They have to agree with Geoffrey Holland, 'If the two year YTS fails then we are at the end of the road. There is nowhere else to go' (*TES* 13/9/85). Indeed, Labour's only real difference with the Tories is that their government would legislate for employers to contribute to the costs of YTS. A position that the Conservatives may yet come to if their repeated exhortations to employers continue to fall on deaf ears. (The MSC has already embarked on a two-year inquiry into the funding of vocational education and training which could lead to compulsory contributions from employers.)

With examples like the Coventry lightbox assembly, however, it is easy to see how the MSC has earned its street name of the Ministry of Social Control; or to assert that youth training schemes teach '. . . not craft skills but rather production line techniques and the "flexibility" and docility appropriate to capitalist development at this stage' (Cole and Skelton 1980: 2). To see what is happening on the ground, how unsuccessful such attempts are, how few young people and their parents believe the advertised claims of YTS and how little attitudes are altered, there are now available a large number of specific studies based upon the experiences of school leavers and trainees. (See especially the Report of the Labour Movement National Inquiry into Youth Unemployment and Training, published by Birmingham TURC, 1987.) But for an overall appreciation of what is happening, there has been sufficient dispute over the numbers enrolling for the scheme in its first year to show how confused the picture is. As *Youthaid's Evidence to the House of Commons Employment Committee* (1985: 9) states, there is '. . . confusion even about the date on which the Youth Training Scheme began. A pilot phase ran parallel with YOP from April to August 1983 after which all new entrants were to YTS, thus the "scheme year" is sometimes taken to start in September, but is more generally referred to by MSC as beginning with the financial year in April. This confusion continues two and three years on as it is unclear when the new two year Scheme will begin (in September 1985 or April 1986).' Training Commission or Manpower Services Commission, at the time of publication it is even unclear what the training agency itself is called and when *or* why the change of name will occur, let alone what will happen to the new Job Training Schemes, or is it the Community Programme (for adults or young unemployed and who is which). (In fact it is the Unified Programme (UP) which is aimed at the young and long-term unemployed and is still voluntary.)

From the announcement of the YTS in the run-up to a general election political claims have obscured a confused reality. In May 1983 *The Observer* reported only 5 per cent of the places on the £1 billion scheme filled. In the same week Norman Tebbit told an election press conference that young people were 'enthusiastically enrolling for the government's new training opportunities'. Come September, national estimates suggested only 40 per cent of places filled. In London, where ILEA colleges had prepared to offer 11,000 places, claims by the MSC of 4,000 signed-up trainees were greeted as wildly optimistic by lecturers. The fate of the many bankrupt small private training agencies shows how confused expectations were.

National figures were massaged as vigorously as those for unemployment as a whole. The MSC claimed that it had anticipated a 20 per cent shortfall in take-up, which it attributed to 'poor advertising and suspicion of the scheme among young people' (*The Times* 13/10/84). But after a Commons reply had elicited that out of 330,000 sixteen-years-olds not in work or full-time education only 220,000 had joined the scheme, David Young was driven to deny that leavers 'preferred the dole' (*TES* 30/3/84). These figures did not include the estimated one in six leaving schemes having joined them and by November 1983 it was revealed that for every person joining YTS two were leaving (*TES* 24/2/84). By April 1984 *The Guardian* reported that of the estimated 340,000 who took some of the 480,000 places available, one in four dropped out within six months. Of 123,000 entrants unaccounted for, MSC admitted that it did not know how many had left, where they had gone or how many had been counted twice because they had moved from one scheme to another. The level of take-up relates to that of unemployment locally; it is lowest in London and the South East (53 per cent) and highest in the North and Wales (84 per cent and 83 per cent). Nevertheless the MSC aimed for 400,000 on the YTS in its second year. MSC's computerization of its counting system in 1984/5 makes comparisons with 1983/4 particularly difficult. However, it is now clear that the total number on one year YTS peaked in October 1984 at 312,832, just 4,000 more than the maximum achieved by YOP two years earlier and 3 per cent more than on the first year of YTS one year previously (Youthaid 1985: 10 and 13). This was approximately one-quarter of the age group, nearly half of whom remained in full-time education at school or FE, while one in eight preferred to sign on for benefits while actively seeking employment (as the conditions of benefit have it). Far from being the shirkers and scroungers of ministerial and media mythology, many of these unemployed youngsters appreciated what some researchers also alleged, that in many instances entering YTS could actually reduce their chances of finding work.

MSC declared the criterion for the success of the YTS to be how many trainees secure employment at the end of it. A criterion that is certain to remain unmet however optimistically the figures are interpreted. The Employment Secretary hailed the results of an MSC sampling of 3,500 leaving YTS between April and July 1984 in nine areas of the country with 56 per cent going into jobs as showing a 'highly encouraging start'. Youthaid described these figures as 'a political fiddle', alleging that 55 per cent of non-YTS youngsters were also in jobs by this time. In 1985 MSC admitted the placement rate had dropped to below half to 48 per cent (just as YOP's placement rate fell as the programme expanded). Like the level of take-up, evidence from the MSC's 1985–6 YTS Leavers' Survey showed a reduction in the chances of finding a job after YTS for young people in areas of high unemployment, those who join with low or no qualifications and for young black people. These are, of course, just the youngsters who, without other employment possibilities, are most likely to be on YTS in the first place.

YTS as a permanent response to the accepted permanence of mass youth unemployment is persistently undermined by the continued aggravation of that unemployment. Training, even if it were all training of high quality, does not of itself produce jobs. MSC's annual report for 1985 shows unemployment moving up the age range to affect those over eighteen as badly as school leavers. All school leavers may be coerced into accepting places but inevitably most will be displaced at the end of their training; especially after the first year of the scheme when it was used by some employers as a means of fulfilling their recruitment needs. As recession deepens, few firms can afford a regular influx of young employees, even ones initially subsidized by YTS. More YTS graduates will therefore rejoin the present half of those under nineteen and quarter of those under twenty-five who are unemployed, while their job prospects are squeezed both by competition from experienced adults and by new batches of subsidized school leavers. Increasingly the process already apparent during the first years of YTS will futher erode the original consensual aims agreed with the TUC as the scheme, together with the MSC's other programmes and initiatives, becomes subordinated to the government's overall political strategy. In essence, as Finn (1984) has summarized, 'This involves using the YTS as part of an attack on the financial autonomy of local authorities; the privatisation of public services; "freeing" employers from legislative constraints; marginalising trade union involvement; undermining comprehensive education; and "pricing" the young back into work.'

Frith (1980: 40) states that '. . . the long term strategy of the MSC is the development of a state run secondary labour market for young workless and temporarily unemployed adults, to enable them to keep their hands fit and disciplined while they wait to enter or reenter the normal labour process'. From the chaotic organization of these projects at local level, it is doubtful whether there is any 'long term strategy' at all; rather it seems the desperate response to an uncontrolled and unforeseen situation. It may be that the series of ad hoc responses may eventually add up to have the effect predicted by Frith, particularly as the MSC pulls together the existing programmes into what increasingly looks like a progression from the TVEI starting for some at fourteen, through 'guaranteed training' on YTS for the rest with YWS as its second year. YWS was then moved up the age range in the form of the New Workers' Scheme, paying £485 million over two years to give £15 subsidies to employers who pay eighteen-to-nineteen-year-olds less than £55 a week and new nineteen-to-twenty-year-olds less than £65. It has since been replaced by the new Job Training Scheme, set to expand to a quarter of a million places from 1987, though subsequently merged with the Community Programe. This is an even cheaper work-for-benefits regime. The anomaly of moving from the second-year YTS rate of £35 a week to return to benefit levels on JTS/CP could easily be obviated by keeping all YTS trainees on benefit rates. The compulsion to join YTS or lose entitlement to benefit points the scheme in this direction. This then ties in with the Fowler Review proposals for lower rates of benefit for those under twenty-five. Finally, there is graduation to Restart and the Adult Programme, where MSC, through its involvement in the 'City Action Teams', has long touted small business as the solution to unemployment.

MSC counters arguments that it engages in social engineering and is bureaucratic and unrepresentative by claiming to be 'responsive to market forces'. Thus, YTS, like YOP, has quickly become increasingly employer dominated. This meant favouring the A schemes on employers' premises when the shortfall in take-up made the college-based B schemes superfluous. Changes in funding for the new two-year scheme reduced the 85,000 Mode B places to 55,000 eligible for a higher rate of support. New 'transitional' funding arrangements paying only for places actually filled require schemes to get employers to contribute to their running costs. Even with this extra cash, 132 schemes catering for disadvantaged youth closed down in 1986 with 2,200 redundancies, most from the voluntary sector. Most of those that remain are dependent upon the transitional funding and will not survive when amounts are reduced in 1987 (see Peck, *et al.* 1986).

That this redirection of YTS away from colleges of FE and special needs schemes towards schemes on employers' premises was perhaps the intention from the start is suggested by Morrison's remark in October 1982 that the 'beauty' of YTS 'for employers is that they will be able to tailor the training to their own needs.' Similarly, Young as new MSC Chairman declared 'The young should be a source of cheap labour because they can be trained on the job.' Writing in *The Director* in April 1983, he made it plain that 'Training should not be confused with education. Training is about work related skills and is intimately concerned with employment. It is for this reason that training in this country must be employer dominated and ultimately employer led.' Advertising for schemes, aimed initially at convincing parents of their worth, also sold them to employers, in the case of Sight and Sound's radio broadcasts as 'tailor made for London's employers'. Employers retain complete control over hiring and firing trainees, who are excluded from

Employment Protection as well as from most of the Race Relations and Sex Discrimination Acts and for whom Health and Safety cover is largely inadequate.

Opposition – or the lack of it

The TUC accepted all this in return for its three seats on the Commission. Bill Keys stated the view of the General Council at the 1983 Congress: that 'The MSC was the concept of the Congress and indeed we fought for it and we got it.' Trade union representatives also have nominal rights on the Area Manpower Boards but their power of veto has been repeatedly overridden. Since the TUC originally agreed to the YOP as part of the Social Contract, the argument that schemes create jobs has continued to influence leaders who do not want to be accused of 'depriving youngsters of a chance'. Trade unions and community organizations wanting to 'do something' about the deteriorating situation of young people then found themselves embroiled in a structure in which they could do no more than legitimate the manipulation of the unemployment figures.

The argument that YTS represents an extension of state educational provision is also favoured by the TUC. YTS can be represented as fulfilling the long-standing trades union policy of day-release for all young workers. The national training to agreed standards that YTS promises is also an old TUC demand. Similarly, the MSC itself was initially welcomed as the central statutory labour market body unions had long been requesting. By remaining involved and only threatening to withdraw, the TUC claims to have mitigated the government's worst excesses, such as Tebbit's initial proposal to cut the benefit of YTS refusers, or the originally suggested £15 training allowance. A further justification for the trades union presence in MSC is that on schemes run by Labour-controlled local authorities significant concessions can be won, such as 'topping-up' of allowances, although only one in ten schemes pay above the basic rate. Eventually however the TUC representatives on the Commission were forced to oppose the work-for-benefit Job Training Scheme. At the time of going to press they are debating whether to withdraw altogether over the government's stated intention to substantially increase the employer representation on the MSC. Whether they do or not will in practice now make little difference, though if they had refused cooperation from the start, most of MSC's programmes would have foundered ignominiously.

From the beginning the reactions of the unions to the YTS were characteristically fragmented. Typically each union acted to defend its members' particular interests and these varied widely. The movement was thus divided from the start. Reaction ranged from total opposition to YTS in general to strong support for particular schemes (see Eversley 1986 on 'Trade Union Responses to the MSC'). The main teaching unions, NUT and NATFHE, both welcomed the New Training Initiative, though NATFHE subsequently changed its position and opposed YTS. The teachers and lecturers at first saw the proposed scheme as a step towards their policy of comprehensive sixteen to nineteen provision, as well as jobs for their members. NUT's only reservation was that the training allowance was too high and might deter sixth-formers from remaining at school!

There is, however, widespread opposition to YTS among the active membership of all unions. The debate in the movement refigures that which occurred in the nineteenth century among the Chartists and others over the state provision of universal elementary education. Initially the role of individual unions nationally and, in certain sectors, locally was critical to get particular schemes off the ground. Thus the TGWU, for instance, blocked the collapse of their existing agricultural apprenticeship into the YTS. The Civil Service unions were also reluctant to operate the scheme. Four major unions (CPSA, UCW, POEU and NGA) declared their outright opposition to it. The NGA, in the front line of employer attempts to wreck union organization through the introduction of new technology, is the most outspoken critic. In other unions several organized workplaces have been able to reject management efforts to introduce YTS.

Critical cooperation rather than outright boycott remains the majority union policy. Approval of schemes has been subject to agreed conditions being met, but union members have found it difficult through the Area Manpower Boards to exercise their rights to inspect and monitor schemes. They do not have the facilities and assistance necessary to fulfil their tasks adequately. Often schemes of which they did not approve have gained endorsement over their heads from national union leaderships. In any case, schemes approved nationally by the Large Companies Unit of the MSC do not have to be endorsed by local AMBs (27 per cent of all YTSs in London, for instance). These, together with all those schemes which did not get trade union approval either because it was not sought or because they are in non-union workplaces (perhaps 40 per cent of Mode A schemes in London), mean that the majority of the capital's YTSs did not gain the supposedly necessary trade union imprimatur. As YTS enters its successive years with schemes being approved 'on the nod' and trade union interest waning further, the proportion is likely to be even higher. In any case, in an internal document dated December 1982, relating to the Community Programme but applying also to the YTS, MSC states: 'We cannot allow trades unions to have a veto on projects'. If unions do try to exercise their right of veto, the document advises that 'the sponsor should be invited to proceed without trade union approval.' So the attendance of trade unionists on the AMBs is quite cosmetic and serves only to legitimate MSC policy. Despite his advocacy of active involvement by trade unionists to pursue 'an alternative policy', Eversley admits: 'It is becoming a bigger and bigger problem to find trade unionists willing and able to serve on Area Manpower Boards' (ibid: 223).

The joint Labour Party/TUC *A Plan for Training* (1984) was designed to deflect any criticism from membership of the leadership's equivocal policy, just as the Party's *Charter for Youth* (1985) aimed to deflect the demonstrations against YTS called by its own youth section into support for a 'socialist' YTS come the next Labour government. Given the present mood of indulgence for the Labour leadership by the British left, suggestions from within the ranks that the YTS does not and cannot work are greeted as 'impractical'. Descriptions of how it really is are dismissed as 'unrealistic'. Suggestions that more than some extra funds, the correction of a few abuses and the right form of words for a policy of equal opportunities are necessary to produce such a 'socialist'

YTS are labelled 'ultra-left'. Thus, only two out of thirteen contributors to a collection of articles edited by Caroline Benn in 1986 actually suggest abolition of the MSC. However much of 'a national disaster' they say MSC's activities have become under Tory misrule, it is suggested that an appropriately left Labour government could return the Commission to popular control. Then MSC could fulfil its fondly imagined original role, as conceived by the TUC, 'to manage employment and help in the process of structured change' (editors' introduction). The alternatives to MSC's present policies, presented by Clare Short MP and others throughout the book, do not recognize the extent to which the MSC has succeeded in substituting 'the right to training' for the traditional union demand for 'the right to work' (described as recently as the Party's 1981 *Programme for Recovery*, as 'a fundamental principle of democratic socialism'). Nor is it acknowledged how far the MSC has kept ahead of its critics by thinking up Labour's policies before Labour can. Thus MSC also 'guarantees', as Labour promises, a two-year programme of education or training. It is already rationalizing certification as demanded by Short; while Lord Young himself pressed his candidacy for the succession to Sir Keith Joseph with the same unified Ministry of Education and Training planned by other contributors.

Flexible training for adaptable skills

For trade unions YTS represents above all real reductions in wages. Conscription onto schemes through benefit-stop and the replacement of permanent jobs by temporary trainees also threaten unions with compulsory labour. A further area of union concern should be with the surrender to the state of all control over training and recruitment into work. The agreed procedures for apprenticeships have been signed away in face of management complaints about 'time serving' and 'restrictive practices'. With the virtual collapse of apprenticeships, unions have had little choice. Yet, unlike apprenticeships, YTS carries no guarantee of future employment and is not concerned with training for real skills in the traditional or craft sense. A few traineeships involve real skill training but most centre on experience in semi- or unskilled work. Thus they reflect the transformation in the labour market which the application of new technology has brought to industrial processes. This had already emptied many apprenticeships of their real content and left them only as 'time serving' exercises. Recognizing this and having no alternative to offer, trades unions have conceded that there is 'a training problem', thus allowing the state represented by the MSC to impose its solution to that problem.

Logically and fully developed, this solution is a radical and comprehensive rationalization of the entire workforce beginning with the youngest entrants to it. Following a 1980 report of the Central Policy Review Staff, in place of training for particular tasks there is a reclassification of the skills needed for a modernized economy into 'competencies' required for eleven 'occupational training families'. Within these families trainees are expected to move in a 'flexible' and 'adaptable' manner.

The notion that all possible tasks involved in every occupation in the economy can be accommodated within eleven training families and that within them the skills required to perform those tasks can be subdivided into different levels of particular skills has been greeted with disbelief and derision. The concept of skill is particularly ill-defined. 'There are in fact no such things as "isolable skills", divorced from the general practice of learning in its proper sense, which can be detached and "taught". For one thing, if British industry, the MSC or DES knows what skills the working population of the twenty-first century are likely to need, they are certainly keeping it a well guarded secret' (Johnson 1983: 19). In a study that the MSC financed but delayed before publishing by the Psychology Department at Warwick University, Annett and Sparrow (1983), clarified much of the semi-technical, pseudo-scientific jargon that MSC has elaborated, together with the Institute of Manpower Studies at Sussex University, around the nature of skills, their acquisition and transferability. They state, 'Occupational Training Families are a device for planning training programmes. They derive more from conventional wisdom than either from psychological theory or from statistical analysis of actual job components. We find no basis in the psychological literature for expecting greater transfer of training between jobs within the same occupational training family than between those which have been classified as belonging to different families beyond what could be expected from an empirical determination of common elements. OTFs might even have an undesirable blinkering effect if people who have received training within one OTF were to regard themselves as unsuited to work in another' (15). Whether or not as a result of this report, OTFs went out of fashion in the higher reaches of the MSC, though schemes continue to be organized along their lines. It seems that 'modularized training' has come to replace them as ideological justification for the Commission's activities (see p. 126 et seq.)

However, this redesignation of skills is exactly the process which occurs when new technology is applied to old industries. For example, in shipbuilding employers' first demand was for an end to 'restrictive practices' and 'demarcations' by workers willing to move 'flexibly' between tasks. The application of new technology had emptied these tasks of their particular complex of skills and rendered them more similar and simple. As the TSA's 1981 *Agenda for Action* put it: 'Britain needs a flexible, adaptable workforce to cope with the uncertainties that cloud the future . . . firms and individuals must either adapt to change or become victims. . . . Individuals will need to be able to adapt to the changing demands of industry, a process which is not once and for all but continuing' (164): adaptability being, as Sarup remarks, 'a synonym for unskilled labour' (1978: 59).

This demand for 'adaptability' and 'flexibility' corresponds with a major reorganization of employment strategy by large firms. They have collapsed around a core group of permanent employees with a large periphery on 'hire and fire' and short-term contracts, agency 'temps', outworkers, self-employed and sub-contractors. These can be expanded or contracted according to demand (see Atkinson 1984). Confusingly, it is for this peripheral labour market that the 103 generic and transferable 'core skills' prepare all YTS trainees. The spread of such temporary working has been rapid: in April 1983, 19.2 per cent of Job Centre vacancies filled were for temporary jobs. By January 1985 this had risen to 38.2 per cent. There has also been an increase in part-time working: 76 per cent of new jobs from 1971 to 1981, 65 per cent of them for women. Similarly, the workforce increased by 480,000 during 1983–4, '. . . the result of a large increase in part-time employment offset by a small fall in the number working full-time' (MSC Labour Market Quarterly Report 3/85). Where YTS preparation for working in this 'demand flexible' environment is most clearly seen as an object of MSC policy is in the Social and Life Skills training that accompanies Skill Training within any particular OTF or module.

Social and Life Skills aim at getting young people to accept their siutation as operatives within a limited range of employment where they will be required only intermittently. Thus they should not anticipate a lifetime of work in one particular occupation (a constant MSC theme). Instead, they should expect to shift from one semi-skilled occupation to another as demanded, with periods of unemployment in between to be used as 'creatively' as possible. The schools having been blamed since the Great Debate for not developing these 'realistic' attitudes in young people, MSC seeks to remedy their deficiency by SLS training. This reinforces the notion that the lack of such social skills in young people themselves is responsible for their lack of employment – typically blaming the victims for their situation. Social and Life Skils are one of the three main components of YTS, along with work experience and instruction in 'broad-based practical skills'.

In Saatchi and Saatchi's advertising for the new two-year YTS, broad-based practical skills are promoted as the subject of the first year's training with specialization for particular skills promised as the substance of the second. This will probably vary from scheme to scheme however. 'Many schemes are not broad based but specifically linked to the needs of the industry or company involved – in some cases to the complete exclusion of sections of the MSC's proposals' (Income Data Services Ltd 1985: 9). An HMI survey of FE courses for YTS found 'attempts to provide a broadly based introduction to a family of jobs were not readily acceptable' (DES 1984: 6). 'There was little evidence of integration or coordination of core skills, vocational studies and work experience' (25) in the 'depressing conditions that failed to provide adequate practical working environments' where in 'many instances' training took place (21).

As for work experience, MSC's own survey of managing agents found 40 per cent of trainees spent most of their time helping other workers to do their normal jobs and another 30 per cent doing work on their own similar to that done by ordinary employees. The remainder, including all apprentices, were involved in systematic on-the-job training unrelated to production. The general principle of work experience has also been queried as 'strange', since 'A few years ago school leavers without qualifications of any kind had no difficulty in getting jobs', whereas, 'Many of them are now deemed to need "work experience" before they can be regarded as employable' (Showler and Sinfield 1980: 117).

Social and Life Skills is the most nebulous of the three component parts of YTS. It has therefore been open to the most dissatisfaction from trainees and criticism from without. Nevertheless few critics note how SLS courses in colleges have developed from the existing provision for special school leavers. (An exception is Steve Bloomhead, a college Vice Principal, writing in Coles 1987.) The MSC's *Instructional Guide to Social and Life Skills* presumes such an identity between the small numbers of special school leavers who have always found difficulty functioning in normal life and who have been helped by colleges to do so and the vast numbers of unemployed youth now drafted into YTS. 'Many people,' it says, 'lack some of the basic day-to-day skills which most of us take for granted. Life skills refer to all those abilities, bits of information, know-how and decision making which we need to get by in life' (1984c: 1). Attitudes and habits are dignified as skills, the lack of these in individuals being responsible for their unemployment. (Though, paradoxically, if Matthews's claim (1963) that most of his sample of educationally subnormal boys could more easily be placed in employment holds true, it is the special school leavers who are better adapted to the demands of modern industry than their more normal contemporaries.)

To compensate for the required skills which are lacking and to fill the compulsory hours of attendance with some practical activities, there is in colleges a proliferation of 'multiskills' workshops, originally used with special schools groups. Here trainees practise a little cookery, joinery, housecraft, mend plugs and replace fuses, etc., and there is reiterated emphasis upon the core areas of literacy, numeracy and some familiarity with computer keyboards. There is little room here to construct an alternative pedagogy, 'which is practically indistinguishable from a skills approach, but to apply it to genuine problems', so as to teach 'Really Useful Knowledge', as Waugh (1982) urges. For MSC has excluded discussion of questions 'related to the organisation and functioning of society in general' and, as their instruction guide continues, 'One of the aims of Life Skills Training will be to adjust trainees to normal working conditions, giving attention to such matters as time-keeping, discipline and the maintenance of relations with others.' Such is 'Life' defined by the MSC. The Business and Technical Education Council has gone along with this, excluding 'General and Communications Studies' from its courses (not only YTS). In any case, with the accelerated moves from colleges to training on employers' premises, the time available for 'Life Skills Training' is further curtailed in favour of acquiring such skills on the job.

New assessments, old divisions

The assessment of SLS, along with any practical skills learnt in whatever training may or may not be provided, has posed a problem for the MSC that is familiar to those who have for long been concerned to extend certification of some sort to the 'lower quartile' of 40 per cent leaving school with no or low examination results. Since the publication of the Further Education Unit's 1979 *A Basis for Choice*, proposals for extension of examination to all have emphasized the virtues of 'accredited experiential learning' for achievements beyond those recorded in conventional written examinations. Here again though, the same sea-change has transformed the terms of a debate that began by attempting to widen opportunities within a still expanding education system. In a situation of contracting real opportunities that certification gives access to this attempt becomes a new tool for manipulation and a new badge of failure.

The attempt to rationalize provision and to develop a meaningful curriculum for non-academic further education can be seen in the competition between the different examining boards to secure for themselves what was anticipated as a lucrative and expanding market. There was also an attempt by the DES, which repeatedly tried to get the competing boards to cooperate with one another, to stave off the MSC's inroads into this area. For here as elsewhere, whoever controls the examinations thereby holds the key to controlling the curriculum. The National Council for Vocational Qualifications was set the impossible task of sorting out the confusion that exists and introducing selected qualifications for accreditation beginning in summer 1987. These are intended to attest standards of practical competence as defined by employers. Supposedly these will be the practical equivalent of academic GCSEs and A levels. Yet Margaret Levy, the Director of MSC and Coombe Lodge's Work Based Learning Project, admitted in *Transition* (7/87), 'There is a possibility that "academic" qualifications will still be given priority in primary selection (for employment) even when a national system ofvocational qualifications is in place. The effect of this would be to down-grade the new national vocational qualifications, even though they provide more precise information of the kind employers say they require.' This 'possibility' is rendered a certainty as Mr Baker's opted-out direct-grant schools revert to a traditional pursuit of academic excellence and top grades in GCSE and A levels under the spur of parental market demand.

Whatever the final form of the new vocational exams, MSC has been slow to apply the results of its researches or those of the Boards to YTS. There have been so many other problems during its first years that perhaps whatever was to happen at the end of it was the last of MSC's concerns. As late as May 1984, Jack Mansell, then Chief Officer of the FEU, wrote in the *TES* 'At present the outcomes of YTS are unclear. They have not been generally agreed except in the most superficial terms and the MSC's own certification of YTS completion certainly presents itself as a most superficial document.' This remains the case, even though the 1985 White Paper proposed a 'recognized vocational qualification' for two years YTS. MSC Commissioners warned at the time that they could not have this ready for 1986, at the same time asking for more than the extra £300 million promised for extending YTS another year. So the scheme entered its fourth year expanded to two years but still without any recognized document of achievement or completion. Imagine the furore if a new two-year course in schools or colleges were launched without any clear idea of what was to be achieved, how it was to be assessed or what the final qualification would be worth! In response to demands for raised standards and following the exposure of the absence of them on particular schemes, the MSC has instituted a Training Standards Advisory Service of thirty to forty inspectors. But 'The basic role of the TSAS will be in-depth surveys of individual schemes. . . . Such surveys would be far less frequent than the normal monitoring visits carried out by MSC staff' (*YTS News* 5/86). The TSAS will thus clearly be inadequate to have any more than a minimal effect upon overall standards of training. Indeed, no scheme has to date been refused the coveted Approved Training Organisation status that secures MSC funding for the next five years. A large number of schemes were only given provisional approval at their first assessment but the MSC could not afford to lose so many of its managing agents by not approving them all. The Construction Industry Training Board, which is the largest of all the agencies, even threatened to withdraw from YTS altogether if it did not gain MSC approval.

The competition to produce validation for prevocational education is essentially an effort to reassert the meaning of a knowledge increasingly perceived as irrelevant; together with the authority of teachers over an education increasingly emptied of content as it moves towards a 'world of work' progressively deskilled by new technology and labour rationalization. At the same time traditional academic criteria, which are teachers' only defence against the utilitarianism of training for work and so come to represent the ideal of education for its own sake, are perceived as increasingly archaic by comparison with what is presented as the chance to obtain what most pupils and their parents want – some sort of work. Teachers' knowledge and expertise does not lie in these new areas but in those of passing the old type of written examinations, which they did themselves and have been taught to teach others to do. So there is a collapse of what Willis (1977: 64) called 'the teacher paradigm', in which the teacher gained control over pupils in exchange for information, that information subsequently being exchanged for qualifications for waged work. This collapse is particularly marked in comprehensive schools with a predominantly working-class intake.

The new structures of education are an effort to contain this growing crisis in schools while at the same time they attempt to meet the contradictory imperative of saving on costs. Certainly the new structures will be critically influenced by the success or failure of YTS. For it is still too soon to say whether YTS can or will become, as Nicholson hoped, 'An important, permanent part of national life which is seen and accepted as the sensible way of progressing from school to work' (*YTS News* 12/85); or whether it will sink into the sands of obscurity once the spotlight of advertising promotion and political expediency has shifted. Sam Whitbread, whose company is one of the most enthusiastic supporters of youth training and other packages to develop 'social and enterprise skills', foresaw the possibility that, if quality is not improved, 'the YTS movement will simply fade over the years' (reported in the *TES* 17/7/87). Nobody doubts that, in the extremely unlikely event of the much promised upturn returning the economy to full employment, the YTS would be quietly forgotten. (Though MSC argues that it is the contribution which only YTS can make to 'reskilling the workforce' and 'pricing the young back into jobs' that is essential for any upturn to occur.)

The future of YTS is still as uncertain as was that of elementary public education when it was first introduced in the nineteenth century. For there was nothing inevitable about the form taken by the modern schooling system that is now taken for granted over a hundred years later. Its introduction was highly problematic and preceded by a prolonged public polemic. The complexity of the debate can be gauged by the fact that universal elementary state schools were opposed not only by the mine and mill owners who feared any extension of education to the mass of the people, but also by Marx who considered that it was better that the workers' children remained illiterate than that they be educated in state schools (1966: 299–300). Today the arguments are just as complex and the situation equally fluid.

CHAPTER 6

Full circle: Towards a new Victorian age of education

Schooling for a post-industrial economy

As the accumulated evidence makes clear, vocationalism as a strategy applied to state education since 1976 can already be seen as as much of a failure as the comprehensive solution it has attempted to replace. Comprehensivization of the secondary schools from 1964 onwards in its turn presented itself as the answer to the failure of the previous tripartite system established by the 1944 Act. The new vocational approach moves towards reinstating this tripartite structure in a new form corresponding to the new divisions of labour in a changed economy. It cannot, however, any more than either the old tripartite schooling or the comprehensives could, create the industrial demand for labour by educating or training school leavers for the skills that are predicted will exist in the future. In this respect vocationalism is a less honest approach to education than the other two main paradigms of the past. The grammar/technical/secondary modern schools openly supposed a continued demand for the non-manual/skilled/semi-/unskilled manual labour traditionally required by industry since before the war. As the economy changed in the 1960s there was a certain amount of wishful thinking in the anticipation that comprehensive schools could produce a better educated workforce for the scientific skills imagined in the future. Now the 'flexibility' and 'adaptability' with which vocational and prevocational education attempts to equip the majority of school leavers may be optimistically presented as the key skills to the modern economy. In practice, however, they represent a dilution of previous skill levels and a preparation for the intermittent, low-waged working that a 'demand-flexible' economy requires.

Vocationalism in education is based on the false premise of the problem of transition from school to work. The problem is presented as one in which the culture of schools no longer corresponds to the attitudes expected at work. It is not the culture of schools that has changed, however. The ways of working in industry now demand different attitudes from different sections of the workforce, allocated by the use of new technology to new divisions of labour. Instead of the old outcomes of schooling for a division of the workforce in the proportions 20:40:40, there is a demand for a new division tending towards the proportions 20:80. While the top 20 per cent continue as before to higher education for non-manual occupations, for the 80 per cent required for intermittent, semi-skilled, peripheral working there is no necessity for a higher educational standard beyond functional literacy and numeracy. This is normally attained in primary school which leaves the secondaries without an agreed role. This was always the case for the 'lower quartile' of pupils who, repeated reports confirmed, found their secondary school experience particularly pointless and irrelevant to their future working lives. This experience is now shared by the next quartile whom the modest certification of good CSEs previously helped into apprenticeships and office jobs that are decreasingly available.

Rather than specific complexes of skills of the type represented by traditional apprenticeship training, it is attitudes not abilities that are critical for successful functioning in the deskilled, so-called 'post-industrial' economy. Personalities that can survive this environment are valued more than increasingly obsolescent mechanical skills. Since such attitudes cannot be taught, even by Social and Life Skills courses, education is being emptied of actual substance. At the same time vocationalism claims to be replacing schools' irrelevant academicism with work-relevant training content. The schools have always been culturally disjointed from the way of life and occupational expectations of the majority of their pupils. The problem was not one of transition from school to work but of more than physical transition into school in the first instance. Increasingly, however, the aspirations for work of most pupils and their parents cannot be met. The problem is not one of transition into work but of work itself.

Vocationalism has no solution for this crisis. Training, even if it were all training in real skills, cannot of itself produce jobs, as the failure of human capital theory in the developed and underdeveloped world clearly shows. It cannot even produce the skills required should a recovery in the demand for labour ever take place. Such skills cannot be developed in a vacuum but must be applied practically in order to develop. Meanwhile the efforts to modernize apprenticeships by abolishing time-serving and instead training for flexible working in place of particular skills, only add to the problem of surplus labour. As seen, even government reports have conceded that the Youth Training Scheme actually increased the unemployment it claimed to be alleviating. Training measures are confused with attempts to meet the threat to social order posed by unemployment. Thus the YTS, which began by proclaiming itself as providing modernized apprenticeships for all, has now reintroduced time-serving with its extension to two years. This time-serving is no longer necessary to acquire the simplified skills required for working the new technology, as three and originally seven years (in the 1503 Statute of Artificers) were needed to learn the skills and culture of a craft. Not only do capital goods have increasingly short lives, but the human capital invested in craft knowledge is also rapidly overtaken by technological change. Instead of shortening apprenticeships to match the short life of specific, limited skills, however, a more rational approach would lengthen learning times to increase real adaptability and transform work into an open-ended education, rather than narrowing education into routine work.

This is not the approach of MSC's utilitarian vocationalism, which is no more capable of solving the present crisis in education and of delivering the workforce needed by the economy in the future than were either of the two previous educational solutions it has superseded. In fact it is a characteristic of the history of educational reform that has been reviewed that none of the three settlements 'in and over schooling' since the war presented a complete and systematically functioning pure type of selection and schooling. Even the 1944 tripartite organization, which appears the most complete and coherent system, was in fact based upon and shaped by the previously existing divisions of elementary and secondary schooling. While, since the beginnings of comprehensivization marked by the 1964 Labour government, it has been the constant complaint of its advocates that comprehensive reform was too slow and remains incomplete. A mixed economy of selective and non-selective schooling continues to exist. Even within and between schools there are varying selective and non-selective elements. To this *mélange* has now been added the tendency towards vocationalizing the curriculum. This latest vocational trend, though it may remain dominant for a time, is also most unlikely to replace its predecessors altogether to establish a complete system of state education, particularly as the Education Reform Bill throws state schooling back to competition for traditional academic standards in the minority of schools that opt out of the state system.

Amidst this confusion of vocationalism with the comprehensive and selective systems of the past and future, certain underlying forces are plainly irreversible. These social and economic determinants establish the conditions in which the mixture of different approaches to education find their particular institutional forms. They also influence the changing relations of one type of schooling to another. The latest applications of new technology are clearly one of the most formative influences upon education in recent years. Their effects can only increase with the exponentially rapid rate of technological change. New patterns of housing consequent upon changing home ownership have heightened the slewing of school intakes by residential segregation. The most important determinant of change, however, is the persistent imperative for the state to centralize control and cut back on funding for public services in response to continuing and aggravated economic decline.

'It is an inescapable fact that some secondary schools will have to close' (Audit Commission Report, May 1986). This is above all an economic imperative beyond the demographic changes that are again swelling numbers in primary schools, while there is a perhaps temporary falling off from the larger numbers of secondary pupils in the recent past. Education and health are highly labour intensive and so it is here that the state can make most savings in its expenditure. Even with a redirection of priorities away from defence spending, additional rationalization would be required sooner or later, as the economy continues to decline, as predicted by all the accepted indicators. (For a not too apocalyptic but nevertheless pessimistic forecast, see Keegan *Britain Without Oil* 1985.) 'Parental choice', enabled by the Education Reform Bill, will provide an ostensibly fair market mechanism to justify closing 'unpopular' or 'unsuccessful' schools. Prior to this, rationalization has already been taking place for some time, as witness the battles against closures of small, 'non-viable' schools. HMI in their 1986 report clearly view six forms of entry as the minimum size for a viable comprehensive school. Sixth forms in comprehensive schools in working-class districts are already a thing of the past, especially in those inner-city areas where Labour-controlled authorities have introduced tertiary colleges. These reinforce the traditional role of sixth-form colleges for academic pupils by combining them with the 'new sixth' of non-academic pupils.

The new pattern of further education following the rise of structural youth unemployment is also now well established. Tertiary modern FE has always had three tiers of students with three distinct pedagogical paradigms. Traditional craft and clerical courses are now being squeezed by academic courses above with students from the decapitated comprehensive sixth forms and the vastly expanded prevocational courses below. The latter have grown out of and hugely augmented the previous traditional provision in colleges for special school leavers.

The prolongation of the teachers' dispute has already loosed market forces to further strengthen the private schools in relation to the state system. Their improved position rendered unnecessary the inclusion of vouchers in the Education Reform Bill or any addition to the Assisted Places Scheme. The biggest increase in pupils for five years was announced in 1986 by the Independent Schools Service, which represents 80 per cent of all private schools. It brought to 6.5 per cent the total of all the country's pupils in private schools. Within the secondary sector, the proportion of private pupils was around 10 per cent; 17 per cent of all sixth-formers. While numbers of fee-paying boarders were down marginally, the increase in largely day pupils was marked, especially for girls (up 4 per cent). Average fees for these schools were £4,000 per annum for boarders, with £254 spent on each pupil per year compared with £30.57 in state schools. The average income of the fathers supporting these children in private schools was £23,494.

Within and between state schools disparities in provision are widening as a result of the steady haemorrhage in funds from repeated cuts. Cutbacks, or merely the failure to match the rate of persistent inflation, entail more reliance by schools upon charitable donations from their parents. This further aggravates the existing advantages of schools in middle-class over those in working-class areas. As a result, as the HMIs report (DES 1985a: 5), 'There are sharp polarisations in provision between schools in different parts of the country and within the same LEA.' These divergencies will be widened by proposals to allow individual schools to manage their own budgets independent of the LEA. This system was piloted in six Cambridgeshire schools during 1986 and extended to all that authority's schools in 1987.

The eventual outcome of this independent budgeting will be to strengthen the position of the 'successful' schools, while the 'market forces' of 'parental choice' will close the least successful. At the same time schools could begin to charge fees for more facilities or 'extras', as the 1987 Education Act puts it. As in the private sector, 'extras' could soon include better equipment, smaller classes and more qualified teachers attracted by higher salaries. Hence Mr Baker's insistence on doing away with nationally negotiated wage rates for teachers, not only because it fits with the government's preference for locally negotiated, 'plant by plant', wage bargaining. In such a system of semi-private agencies each will receive government grants according to the number of pupils it attracts (as the MSC funds managing agents per trainee on YTS). With headteachers as managing directors accountable to a board of governors made up of parents and local industrialists, LEAs will have virtually no role. Through systematic tests at seven, eleven, fourteen and sixteen central government will monitor the attainment of the minimal objectives it lays down in a national core curriculum. These tests will also provide an indication of the 'success' or otherwise of the schools to parents and of the performance of their teachers to heads. Private schools could have no objections to joining such a state system in which they, like all schools, would be able to select pupils and charge fees. In return, they would receive government grants for every pupil they already have. In fact this happens already in the allocation of pupils to private schools through the Assisted Places Scheme. Such is Mr Baker's vision of the 'new partnership between parents and the state'.

Meanwhile the condition of many buildings continues to deteriorate so that often the environment is shabby and uninviting. There has in fact been no improvement overall in the state of school buildings since 1981. Increasingly parents are being asked to provide their children with the books and equipment they need. While the threats to finally terminate the already reduced school meals service, if carried out, will end the one square meal that is all that many poor children receive. Although, as the HMIs conclude, most schools are not yet falling down, leaking or facing crises in the availability of materials and equipment, 'Many schools are being affected in these ways, and many teachers and pupils working in depressing conditions with inadequate resources' (ibid.: 12).

Cuts in higher education, where there was a savage pruning of student numbers in 1981, have already accentuated the mismatch between industry's needs and educational provision that it has been the object of government policy to avoid. At a time when competitor countries are expanding their university intake, there are specific shortages in engineering and information technology at graduate level. Paradoxically there are also unfilled places on several engineering degree courses. The situation will worsen as the effects of the cuts continue to work their way through. They will also have an impact on secondary schools in precisely those areas of science and computing supposedly required by modern industry. There is already such a shortage of qualified mathematics, science and CDT teachers that a crash training programme will be necessary if the UK is ever to catch up (see DES 1985b).

The TVEI

Disparities within and between secondaries are also heightened by central government initiatives such as the Lower Attaining Pupils' Project and the Educational Support Grants. LAPP will be the English contribution to the second phase of the EEC pilot projects on the transition from school to work (see page 73), for which £2 million will be available from the EEC or through the Urban Programme. ESGs follow the pattern of tying the allocation of central funds to certain specified objectives of local authority provision. But it was the MSC's Technical and Vocational Educational Initiative for fourteen-to-eighteen-year-olds which all available studies agree caused the widest differences between the schools in which it was piloted and the rest.

Like YTS, 'The TVEI embodies the Government's policy that education should better equip young people for working life' (HMSO 1985a). There is a certain vagueness about the skills with which TVEI aims to equip its pupils. These were stated by MSC to be both 'transferable' and 'specific'. But TVEI is generally directed towards new technology, business studies and teaching about particular, local industries. It was suddenly announced by Mrs Thatcher in answer to a planted Parliamentary question in November 1982 without the usual formal consultation with education authorities. £46 million was immediately promised over five years for pilot schemes in fourteen LEAs. By January 1984 this was expanded with an additional £100 million for sixty-two authorities. By May 1985 only twenty-four authorities were not bidding to take part. TVEI thus provides a striking example of MSC's style of rapid operation. As the then Chairman David Young explained in *The Times* (22/11/82), 'Supposing we had decided to launch a debate about technical education or the lack of it. We might have had a Royal Commision or it might have taken five years or even ten to get off the ground. Now we have a pilot project due to start by September next year.'

The launch of TVEI also showed the cooperation that was

for a time characteristic between Young ('the only man', Mrs Thatcher said, 'who brings me solutions and not problems'), Tebbit (then Minister of Employment and therefore nominally head of the MSC), Joseph (then Education Secretary) and the Prime Minister herself. Until Sir Keith's departure and the subsequent feuding between Tebbit and Young, it was this 'Gang of Four' that really made policy in the crucial area of education and training. As a former property developer who failed in business in the USA, returning to head the Conservative Party research unit and advise Sir Keith at the Department of Trade and Industry, Young's only qualifications for doing so seem to be that he was for a time the British Director of the Organisation for Rehabilitation and Training. ORT is a Jewish charity, now operating in thirty-two countries, which began in Tzarist Russia training unemployed youth. Its approach is narrowly utilitarian and its trade schools in France seem Young's immediate inspiration for TVEI. ORT was subsequently involved in planning curricula for the City Technology Colleges that succeeded TVEI as the government's main technical education venture in schools.

There was some confusion at first over whether the TVEI would exclude the academically able. Lord Young at first said that it would, but the MSC quickly clarified that the initiative was open to all. It was in fact by its nature a selective programme. It involved only some pupils in some schools. Schools, or the selected streams of pupils within schools, receiving the massive injections of MSC money benefited from new equipment, better staffing and resources over those without. Clwyd, the only LEA which attempted to introduce TVEI into all its secondary schools, was soon told by MSC to restrict its spending to the 250 designated pupils in its five TVEI schools. Capitation (the grant to a school based on its number of pupils) for each TVEI pupil was four times that allocated to non-TVEI pupils. In their concentration upon technical skills, TVEI pupils drop wider areas of science and other subjects save the core areas of English and mathematics. There is evidence that in a number of schools TVEI thus stunted other parts of the curriculum, such as history, geography and modern languages. Competition between departments and between schools, already a life and death matter in a situation of falling rolls, was heightened by the selective injections of TVEI funds. But TVEI offered one of the few remaining routes to career promotion for many teachers, who therefore welcomed it if with reservations (see NUT and NAS statements on TVEI).

Like YTS, TVEI proclaims itself a transitional programme, from school to work, fourteen to eighteen. Despite MSC 'advice' to LEAs not to reveal their figures, indications from the pilot schools are that around two-thirds of the pupils who signed on the programme at fourteen left at the normal age of sixteen. Only in Birmingham, where there was a particularly rapid collapse of job opportunities and where YTS was notoriously bad, did a majority (65 per cent) stay on to complete their TVEI at eighteen. As reported in the *TES*, 'In many cases the percentage of youngsters staying on appears to be little different from the normal average in their authority' (1/11/85). Wigan claimed a 40 per cent staying-on rate as an achievement because a high proportion of their TVEI pupils were low attainers. 'We never expected to get anything like a majority of the youngsters staying on. That will not happen until the programme is able to attract high achievers and there can be no question of that until they are offered a chance of obtaining the kind of qualifications that they and their parents value.' (ibid)

Schemes vary widely in different schools and in different authorities. In some it appears that TVEI streams within schools creamed the most able pupils, while in others they were used as a dumping ground for lower attainers. In others, they offered the middle quartile promises of employment in the 'proper' or 'good' jobs they have lost. Overall there were from 58 to 42 per cent more boys than girls on TVEIs. Boys were concentrated in technical studies, including microelectronics, and the girls in business studies and catering. Also overall, black pupils seemed less likely to take part than white. In addition, Maurice Holt, in his wide-ranging assessment of the Initiative (1987), notes that no independent school has shown any interest in adopting TVEI. The same could be said for all vocational and prevocational programmes and assessments. Nor has the government made any extra funds available to the private sector for this purpose.

Announced at its inception by Norman Tebbit as 'the rebirth of technical education' (*The Times* 13/11/82), the 3 per cent of all pupils in TVEI appeared to fit into a new typology of reinstated tripartite education. After an eleven to fourteen 'banded' or 'set' curriculum, the usual top 20 per cent continued as ever to prepare for traditional examinations at eighteen for entry to higher education. In a reduced middle band those on TVEI followed this modern reincarnation of a technical high school course. The majority meanwhile combine a core curriculum with social and life skills and work experience as they prepare for transition to the two-year compulsory YTS from sixteen to eighteen. Instead of 20:40:40 moving towards 20:80, the pattern may thus be 20:3:77. This pattern would be the same if City Technology Colleges replaced TVEI to supply technical education. (Or rather, would approximate to 20:0.45:79.55, since there are so few CTCs, even on paper.)

The outcome of this particular experiment doomed for success, as TVEI has been called, is still unclear however. Moon (1983) noted the tendency of government pilot schemes in response to unemployment to become the basis for further policy developments. In other words, money taken from cuts elsewhere is thrown at the problem without any clear idea of what will happen thereafter but in the Micawberish hope that 'something will turn up'. The brake upon further development of technical training via the TVEI is the prohibitive cost of equipping and staffing the programme. It is difficult to see therefore how it can be extended to all schools as intended, unless it were funded directly by employers themselves. Since it is still far from obvious to most employers that TVEI will provide them with their future labour needs (where these can be predicted), it is most unlikely that they will willingly contribute to training of doubtful utility, especially when hard-pressed for funds themselves. MSC's five-year grants to develop TVEIs were intended as 'pump priming' to get schemes started and no more. The last extension of the scheme, announced in a 1986 White Paper, provided £90 million for all secondary schools, over ten years. This has been calculated as sufficient only for three-quarters of a teacher extra in each school. This extension of TVEI is in fact an admission of the Initiative's failure. Although it generalized MSC influence to all schools, that influence was spread much thinner even if wider. For the original intention was that TVEI would be extended to all schools not by further government grants but by contributions from employers that have not yet been forthcoming. To this dilemma City Technical Colleges, which concentrate all resources in a few inner-city centres, present an answer. They represent an attempt to sustain with diminishing resources an increasingly contradictory and confused policy for education and training and another admission of the failure of previous efforts. They also offered a model for the direct-grant-funded schools that the Education Reform Bill would allow to opt out of the state system.

Modules and profiles

The modular structure of TVEI assessment and examination supposedly facilitates transfer to whichever different qualifications are selected in school, college or YTS for those pupils remaining in the programme. Many youth training schemes and the profiled Certificate of Prevocational Education, which was piloted in Northern Ireland as the end certification for the Youth Training Programme there, are also now modularized. In fact, modularization, by which a trainee can accumulate units in one area before transferring to another, seems to have replaced the Occupational Training Families in the planning and structure of YTS. MSC has developed an 'occupational skills inventory' or 'matrix', having sent two officials to Canada and the USA to review the latest applications there of behavioural industrial psychology (see MSC 1977). It has since been developed in collaboration with the Institute of Manpower Studies at Sussex, the Social and Applied Psychology Unit at Sheffield University and the Tavistock Institute.

As summarized by Moore (1985: 5), 'The skills inventory purports to represent skills actually required in industry and necessary to the performance of specific jobs. These skills are represented in the form of atomised "items" of behaviour which can be referred back to underlying "generic skills" and grouped together into Occupational Training Families of associated skills and job clusters. Possession of these skills (referred to as "skill ownership") is seen as facilitating labour mobility by virtue of their "transferability" and so overcome "labour market rigidity" (ie: trade-union "restrictive practices"). A crucial aspect of the skills inventory is that it is immediately translatable into a curriculum because it specifies in a very precise way what people are meant to be able to do (not know) in order to perform particular jobs. Also, because these skills are supposedly drawn directly from industry itself they are taken as representing what employers actually require, hence promoting employability.' From this description it can be seen that by combining transferable skills with the additional, job-specific skills that may be peculiar to a given OTF, modular profiling can assess everything. Modules cover the core area where maximum adaptability and such general attributes as 'problem solving' and 'learning to learn' are stressed in terms that indicate attitudes rather than abilities (rather like the ill-defined but all-pervasive notion of 'general intelligence' formerly rated by IQ tests). As well as this, modules also define and assess the various add-on profiles of the different, job-specific, Occupational Training Families.

More familiarly to educationalists, modules are what the constituent parts of syllabi covered by traditional examinations used to be called. In the USA they have long been the building blocks of degree courses that combine elements of different disciplines: literature, art appreciation and history into 'Renaissance studies', for instance. They are similarly used by the Open University. However, modules are not merely the parts of a whole. As defined by the CPVE Joint Board, 'The term "module" describes a set of experiences and outcomes which may be achieved through a variety of appropriate learning methods.' In assessments (rather than examinations) like the CPVE various modules lend themselves to 'skills profiling' and are bankable in different combinations by individual students. As the Further Education Unit puts it in its own peculiar language: 'modularization' should not be seen as 'a sequential division of the curriculum' but 'as a series of free-standing learning objectives with "build up" effect accruing to the trainee who took them'.

In the ILEA's Hargreaves Report and in some other LEAs, like Clywd, where alternative methods of assessment to conventional examinations are being piloted in schools, modules are known as 'units'. The traditional two-year O level or CSE courses are deconstructed into between eight and ten six- to eight-week units. By combining fourth and fifth years together, individual pupils can pick various routes through the many modules on offer. As long as certain core areas are covered, individuals can choose different combinations to suit their abilities and inclinations. This affords a possible way to prepare previously streamed and separated students for a unitary GCSE examination (but with questions and project work suitable for different levels of ability). It also prepares the majority of pupils to transfer into non-advanced further education, where their records of achievement in secondary school will be recognized and banked as contributions towards generalized pre-vocational courses.

While there is a gain in flexibility and individual choice (and in management ability to control the situation), what is lost in this deconstruction of whole subjects into their constituent parts is any sense of the particular disciplines of previously discrete subject areas. It may be that, save at university level, there was in any case in schools little apprehension by most pupils of different subject specialisms. Even in higher education the boundaries between different disciplines are notoriously irrational and ill-defined. There is certainly a need to unite various areas of enquiry into larger interrelations. Empirically picking and choosing items from the fractured wholes of traditional curricula will not of itself produce such new conceptions. Rather, the units that are accumulated need not be related to each other by any more than their practical similarities. The only unity imposed upon the different combinations of modules available is the student's individual choice informed by the counselling of his personal tutor. That choice is likely to be guided by vocational opportunity. Indeed, the entire system is supposed to be uniquely responsive to employers' needs and flexible enough to meet changes in them by the addition of new modules. There has thus been a loss of abstract conceptualization, relating one area of learning to another, in favour of practical application to particular tasks not necessarily related one to another.

In the two-year YTS, core competencies will be built into

pre-vocational courses that begin with a general introduction to the world of work. Trainees then move more or less quickly through a range of job tasters into other 'experiential learning situations' where work experience familiarizes them with the demands of different work environments. Since the work is not specialized, the skills which it requires can be transferred to other areas, having been demonstrated in practical tests and accredited as part of a profile. Youth training thus moves away from time-serving where apprentices over a given period mastered (for they were mostly young men) the various aspects of a craft, towards a situation where a person can train in just one aspect of a wider occupational activity.

The MSC takes the same approach to its Adult Training, where retraining may only be required to perform one particular task rather than all the possible jobs someone in that occupation might previously have been able to tackle: for example (from the Road Transport Industry Training Board's modularized scheme), the competence to fit exhausts in a drive-in centre rather than all the skills of a qualified mechanic in a garage. Of course the route to further training is not thereby closed. Time and an employer permitting (and these could be crucial), bricklayers accredited only with modules in laying bricks in straight lines may take more modules to build corners, construct cornices and so on. If these more advanced skills are required they will have profiles to show their competence to perform them. If they are not, it is of course extremely unlikely that anyone will pay or be paid to undertake them. Advocates of modular training claim it is more open for individual opportunity, as well as being more flexible and adaptable to industry transformed by the application of new technology, than rigid demarcations between skilled and unskilled work.

It is doubtful, however, that modular training can actually raise the overall skill level of labour. It is more likely that existing skill levels will be depressed by this method of training. Higher-level skills will be lost instead of being preserved and extended in the new circumstances to which they could have been applied. Following suggestions by Pye (1968), skill can be defined as the ability to manage uncertainty rather than (as in modular training) the 'competence' to complete a given task with the certainty demonstrated in a test situation. It can then be seen that the most skilled operations are those requiring complete knowledge of an entire process and the ability to relate understanding of working in one area to comprehend what is happening in another.

Apart from very specific skills involving delicate operations where the most complete knowledge possible of tools and materials is also required (e.g. in traditional handicrafts), the skills most highly valued by society are diagnostic ones. The mechanic, who can test and analyse a car engine to find its faults and repair them, is obviously more skilled than the above fitter who completed only sufficient modules to refit an exhaust. The more complex the machinery or system with which the analyst is able to deal, the more uncertainty there is built into it and the more skill is required to set it up. Thus, in computing, systems analysts, who devise and test new programmes, use more and higher-level skills than the operators who merely follow the system once it has been installed. This also applies to scientific discovery and artistic creation, work that may at the same time use extremely sophisticated equipment, while involving a high degree of theoretical abstraction often combined with creative intuition. In medical science, dealing as it does with the most complex organic systems and the uncertainties of their interrelations and possible malfunctions, surgery is acknowledged as particularly skilful because it combines particular manual skills, using delicate tools on sensitive material, with general diagnostic ability. The manual skills of the proverbial brain-surgeon, including the use of tools such as saws and drills, are no longer derided as they once were ('old saw bones', etc.). Like the tasks of the skilled mechanic, computer systems analyst, scientist or artist, complex surgery combines mental ability acquired through theoretical study with manual dexterity developed by long practice. Neither purely bookish knowledge (things that can be read or said but cannot be done), derived from the abstractions of previously formulated experience, nor the unformulated but tacit knowledge of the practice of a craft ('things that we know but cannot tell', Polanyi 1962), are alone sufficient to manage the considerable uncertainties involved in any of these tasks. The highest order of skills therefore combine mental and manual abilities; as in the first industrial revolution which was made possible, wrote Rosenbrock (1977), by 'the marriage of intellectual inquiry and practical skill'.

Similarly, skill is generally equated with management (in so far as mangement is not, in the words of a Lucas aerospace worker quoted in Cooley (n.d.: 80), merely 'a command relationship, a sort of bad habit inherited from the army and the church'). Although managers may no longer be able, as the old iron masters of the industrial revolution were, to perform all of the tasks of any of their operatives, they are responsible for handling the combined uncertainties of all the various operations undertaken by the organization. Managers lack the skills commensurate with their responsibilities to the extent that they lack an adequate conception of the overall function and direction of their enterprise within its existing constraints. It is precisely this skill of interrelating the various parts to the process as a whole that is lost in the empirical application to isolated tasks unrelated to one another.

'Competence', defined as the certain ability to complete a given task, is different from skill. Eliminating uncertainty from a particular operation reduces it to its simplest, binary terms. Either the operating light shows, in which case press proceed key, or it does not in which case do not proceed / replace the whole unit / call the supervisor. The disasters of this rigid compartmentalization become clearly apparent in the case of what computer scientists call a systems breakdown. Since each operation is simplified to the point of either/or, on/off certainty, their coordination has to be highly synchronized. Breakdown of the system as a whole can then be caused by the failure of any one particular part to operate at its appointed time and order. Once this has occurred there are very few people who still have the overall command of the process to discover and right the fault. Furthermore, the rigidities of such a system make it unable to deal with any change beyond the parameters it has been set. Since change occurs constantly, and in today's technology with exponential rapidity, such a modular approach to training for the future needs of industry is potentially disastrous. It devalues those particularly human skills of intuition and creativity that are irreplaceable by machinery and so often necessary to cope with the uncertainties of unprecedented change. They are being lost in favour of purely mechanical, repetitive and quantifiable certainty.

Skills testing for certain competence, its advocates argue, gives credit for abilities untested by traditional written examinations. All pupils 'can do' at least some of the items profiled on the menu of practical tasks. Their sense of worth is enhanced by their achievements in a test situation, instead of being failed by a comparison with a minority of their peers. Of course, even in a list of practical tasks that are supposedly equivalent to one another, certain items are recognized by both pupils and their teacher as higher-order abilities than others. For example, from an RSA profile for a diploma in communications, the ability to 'Read simple printed texts' is subsumed in the item 'Read complex printed texts', which will be recognized as an objectively higher order achievement – whatever satisfaction a pupil only beginning to read or to learn English as a second language may or may not have gained by recording the more elementary skill. Similarly in another RSA profile in mathematics, the ability to 'Add whole numbers' is subsumed in the higher-order 'Multiply whole numbers', and that again and many other levels of mathematical order in, say, 'Treat first order differential equations in any number of variables' (an item not actually on the profile). Just as, less demandingly but more revealingly, the ability to write an essay or read a book all the way through is not included on the CPVE profile.

Enthusiasts for such skills testing sometimes make the comparison with the long established Ministry of Transport driving test for road users. Considering the numbers of road accidents every year, this is perhaps not a very happy comparison. However, as one of the major, and often the only examinations or tests taken by most people after they leave school, the result of which is completely unprejudiced by their previous school performance, the driving test illustrates the virtues of open accessibility urged for the new skills tests. There is little stigma attached to failing a driving test; you just take it again until you pass. It is an almost completely skill-specific test: either you can perform a three point turn, do an emergency stop and all the other items that the examiner ticks off as they are accomplished in the test situation, or you cannot. Some knowledge of the highway code is also required, tested by traditional question and answer. Thus the driving test indicates the ability to drive to the required standard for what is considered safe road use. What it does not test is any general knowledge about the history and development of transport, the principles of the internal combustion engine, how to repair a motor vehicle or any first aid. Nor should it reasonably be expected to. Such more theoretical knowledge might be required of traffic planners and engineers, while there are other (more or less practical) tests for the more specialized tasks of motor mechanics and ambulance crews. But this is the point that the critics of skill-specific tests are making. They allege that such tests measure only behaviour in narrow test situations. They are restrictive to very specific tasks and exclude others that are related to them. They also obviate the need for the more general and abstract knowledge which is left to the experts and managers who control the process as a whole. Though whether traditional examinations that fail the majority of their entrants, which are all that most critics can offer in the place of the new profiled skills tests, prepare people any better for knowledge about and control over their work and their environment is also doubtful.

With the new criterion-referenced skill tests, as with the old norm-referenced examinations, who sets the questions determines what is to be learnt, or the items to be achieved on the profile making up the particular module. The MSC has stressed all along, as Geoffrey Holland told the CBI (17/1/86), 'It is employers who must say and heavily influence what standards of competence are to be and how they are to be defined. It is employers who determine recruitment practices and beyond this, expectations of the performance of education and training providers.' This is the logic of vocationalism. Any notion of a general or critical education is replaced by learning the tasks required for employment. Similarly, the 1980 Think Tank Report (see page 106) envisioned employer-defined, low-level 'competencies' replacing time-served apprenticeship criteria in the New Training

Initiative. Tasks were to be broken down into their constituent parts and the different skills required to perform them validated in test situations. This unprecedented application of industrial Taylorism seems to have escaped the notice of profiling enthusiasts.

Profiles may even be applied to assessing teachers' completion of their own tasks in similar checklisting manner if the employers are successful in writing a commitment to regular assessment into contracts. Along with other 'Victorian values', it is possible that teachers could again be paid by results as in the nineteenth century. Teacher performance might be measured against the numbers of their charges passing or failing the graded tests of ability at seven, eleven and fourteen which Mr Baker advocates. Notwithstanding that there are serious inherent difficulties about setting age-related objectives when individual pupil performance varies so markedly, these tests were piloted in Croydon. Nationally they would enable simple comparisons to be made between different teachers, classes and schools. This would afford easy monitoring of and secure compliance with the new national core curriculum. Nor need this sort of surveillance necessarily be restricted to schools. A junior education minister recently suggested that judging the performance of polytechnic lecturers would need 'some sort of civilised, gentlemanly, overt system of espionage by consent' (reported in *New Society* 13/6/86). Annual appraisals of performance such as are proposed have already become routine for employees of Marks and Spencer where 'the immediate supervisor fills out a detailed form giving an opinion of how well, or badly, the employee is doing the job. The form is carefully tailored to match each job. A middle manager might be assessed on commercial awareness, but a sales assistant on customer relations. The employee is shown the completed form and invited to discuss it. An interview follows at which both the manager and the employee agree on a written statement which is a fair summary. Although there is no automatic promotion system, merit bonuses are available and could be paid to staff whose assessments prove particularly favourable' (*TES* 8/3/85).

Profiling as an extension of and alternative to traditional examinations has a vast lobby. From the MSC's planned assessment of YTS, this extends to Mrs Williams's advocacy of the abolition of traditional sixteen-plus examinations – 'the biggest single barrier to achieving a classless society,' as she told the SDP's 1984 Education Conference – and their replacement with profiles, school assessments and graded tests. While Labour Party education policy since the Great Debate includes, within its calls for universal access to post-compulsory education, increased vocational and training relevance assessed by 'new forms of examination' (Labour Party 1981). All these approaches see profiles as means to '. . . assess work-related knowledge and skill and which constitute more genuine occupational qualifications', as Hargreaves expressed it (1982: 181). They all therefore accept, as does the TUC, that 'problems' of training and attitudes exist which education is able to remedy. These are not conceived as problems created by the latest tendencies of industrial development. The erroneous assumptions of two distinct worlds of school and work are reaffirmed and perpetuated, while the extension of school or college which they all propose is not recognized as a further prolongation of a dependent state of non-adulthood and exclusion from productive employment. This might not matter if real benefits were to accrue, but the proposed 'work relevant' courses are hardly intended to confer on the majority of youngsters the prolonged dependence and licensed freedom enjoyed by a minority of college students. Rather, these profiled courses are a preparation for the flexible disciplines of intermittent, semi-skilled labour. (Further on profiles, see Ainley 1987.)

Alternative uses of new technology

The tragedy is that new technology need not be applied in this way to further divide people from one another. Rather, it has the potential to simplify, share and integrate their endeavours, increasing productivity with less laborious and repetitive effort. The development of technology presents real opportunities for a transformation of the old division of labour between workers by hand and by brain. Even in the present economic environment, computer-integrated manufacture, which is the logical extension of the computerization presently being applied piecemeal to production, potentially integrates the work of all employees in an enterprise. While it requires fewer operatives (or the same numbers for less time) by storing information centrally it ensures that it is communicated to all. The more inputs there are to the system from designers, engineers and managers, through repairs and maintenance workers, plus those involved in storage and delivery, to sales and marketing staff, the more information is generated and the more effectively it can be integrated for decision making that may also be computer aided. 'The computer answers queries put to it by the operating personnel regarding the short-run effects of variables at various control levels, but decisions are made by the operators. Operating personnel are provided with technical calculations and economic data, conventionally only available to technical staff, that support learning and self-regulation. In this manner operator learning is enhanced' (Hirschhorn 1984: 2). One part of the manufacturing process cannot act without informing and influencing all the others. The more divisions between those who know and those who do are effaced by everyone contributing and sharing information through the computerized communications network, the more responsive can the industry become to the demands of consumers and the needs of society.

The fact that new technology is not applied in this way but is used to rationalize production, usually at labour's expense, shows how little all the training and retraining that it has stimulated is to do with its most productive and fulfilling use and how much to do with reinforcing social divisions of labour and control. One indication of this was the way MSC 'inadvertently allowed' the Civil Service Commission, which recruited its inspectors for the new Training Standards Advisory Service (see p. 112), to classify these posts as 'work that is vital to the security of the state'. Ironically, this excluded from applying for posts as inspectors supposed to confer Approved Training Status upon youth training schemes that comply with, among other things, ethnic and equal opportunities guidelines, those who were not 'assimilated, long-term residents of the UK'.

Consumption utilizes new technology in some ways differently from production. For those who can afford them, increasingly simplified consumer durables perform more and more sophisticated tasks. Equipment that was only a short time ago available solely to specialists is now purchaseable in every high street: computers, video-cameras, synthesizers, hi-fi, mixing and recording studios, do-it-yourself tools, sports equipment and all the gadgetry of kitchen and garden. Often these consumables are only sold in order to be consumed in use and so cannot be easily repaired for instance. But there is in consumption a levelling-up of skills across a range of activities corresponding with the levelling down of skills within a narrowing occupational specialization that occurs with the application of new technology to production. So individualized consumption demonstrates the potential of the new technology for lightening and diversifying labour, fulfilling in part the old dream of '. . . the fully developed individual, fit for a variety of labours, ready to face any change of production, and to whom the different social functions that he performs, are but so many modes of giving free scope to his own natural and acquired powers . . . [who is] "less of a molusk and more of a man" ' (Marx 1889: 493–4).

Mass production is now becoming flexible enough to create personally customized commodities for the individual consumer. Short production runs and miniaturized equipment appear to be reversing the seemingly inevitable tendency towards larger and larger aggregations of workers and machinery in factory production, at least in the developed countries. So much so that a future of 'ownwork' has been predicted (Robertson 1985) in which all work will be undertaken by individuals in the local and household sectors. Similar prophecies of a 'post-industrial society' are made in the common conception of an 'information society', where individuals somehow gain the means to life by swapping information with each other 'telematically' through a 'network architecture' of 'integrated systems' (Williams 1985). The lucky information workers can carry their 'workstations' with them and work wherever they are, in the car, on the beach, at home, transmitting and receiving signals through terminals as small as a wrist-watch. According to the latest Labour Force Survey (1986), self-employment is certainly increasing, mainly in the fields of distribution, services and construction, to 12 per cent of all employment (80 per cent of whom are single persons, i.e. without employees). But self-employment cannot offer the prototype of employment for the majority in the future, save in the sense of an even greater expansion of home-working and peripheral subcontracting. Conditions of most home workers, in the clothing trade for example, are hardly comparable with those of the self-contracting computer programmers, journalists, researchers and accountants, who seem the model for an 'ownworking' or 'information' society.

The idea of a future 'leisure society' in which new technology is so developed that it affords work to only a very few, or for everyone only for a little time, similarly misconceives the trends of present development. Generally such forecasts envision a state-guaranteed basic income and an erosion of the work ethic to end the dependence of wages upon employment, for example Sherman (1986). But productive work is not only, as it is for the majority in present society, the sole means to an income above the poverty level guaranteed by basic social security provision. It is also a prime necessity of life, a human need to act upon and transform the environment. Also, it is not as if there is already no more work still to be done. The decaying infrastructure of Britain's Victorian cities, the thousand and one human wants crying out to be met, let alone the deteriorating ecosystems of the countryside and the destruction, disease and destitution that are destroying so much of the Third World, all require more investment both in labour and in the developed products of the latest technology than ever before. Yet the future that is offered by prophets of the new leisure age, or of post-industrial 'service society', is not one of such real work but rather of a hedonistic self-fulfilment at the expense of the exploited majority in the world.

After the Big Bang

Manufacturing industry, if not of the old, intensive, factory type, must still play a large part in the future of work, simply because even expanded service industries can never export enough to satisfy the demand for imports of both manufactured goods and raw materials. The idea that the industrial revolution has been completed ushering in a new era of 'post-industrialism' is also misconceived. The original industrial revolution created not only a new working class but also a new class of industrial capitalists. Now it is supposed that the end of industrialism spells 'Farewell to the Working Class' (Gorz 1982). Yet, as these writers are the first to admit, when they see their plans for income equalization and work-sharing frustrated by events, the same class that owns the multinational companies and banks which developed from the original industrial revolution remains very much in control. In fact its control is everyday expanding to new areas.

A merger of banking with insurance, retail sales with productive investment and marketing speculation has resulted from the deregulation of the City's financial dealings. Since the Stock Market Crash of October 1987 the 'Big Bang' looks more like a 'Big Bubble'. When it finally bursts it can be expected that even larger agglomerations of all the aspects of business from investment to marketing will survive over their competitors as monopolies managing whole aspects of life. This will facilitate 'moneyless shopping' and the combination of banks/shops/garage/entertainment complexes offering their all at the touch of a credit card. Whether such service industries can compensate for the loss of Britain's industrial base is doubtful. The 'moribund capitalism' of the 'Big Bang', where the speculation in capital becomes more important than the production of any actual goods, may not maintain its profits in the face of increased foreign competition and penetration of the home market.

In this, more likely, future there is little room for the self-development of the ordinary person through expanded education and leisure activities that all the above accounts argue will be necessary. Instead of more information about, control over and participation in society (which new technology also makes possible) the average person in the street is likely to see less. Knowledge and information will be increasingly restricted by the heightening divisions of labour between those who know and those who do. The present trends in education that have been reviewed cannot counter these developments. In fact, vocational pedagogy, limiting any general education more and more to specific training, encourages such a constriction of vision and atrophy of thought. While the selective and competitive tendencies encouraged by Mr Baker's bill can only reinforce a sense of failure in the majority. In any case, the dominant tendency of society is supported by all the apparatus and ideology of consumerism against which the schools have for so long fought a losing battle. Rather, the likely confused shape of education to come that has been predicted will only further reinforce the role of schools in confirming the brainlessness of the many, while selecting the few for positions of management and control.

Crude and direct selection to better educational opportunities for those who are able to pay for them has been predicted as the inevitable result of applying the market forces of 'parent power' to state schooling. The parents who care enough to get their children into the new, direct-grant schools that opt out of local authority control will want them to follow the largely traditional, academic courses leading to entry to higher education and the secure, professional and managerial, core jobs to which these give access. Meanwhile the majority in underfinanced schools, struggling against the consequences of multiple deprivations, will follow the reduced minimum of a national curriculum. Their pupils will prepare on pre-vocational, practical, profiled courses for entry to compulsory YTS/UP. Such a preparation for a future of semi-skilled, intermittent, low-wage, manual labour will figure a very poor second to the academic education offered in the opted-out schools. State-supported at first, these will inevitably come to rely more and more upon fee-paying to sustain them. Payment for different schooling would perpetuate the widening material inequalities in the working population and fracture the cultural homogeneity of the working class (as suggested p. 15).

This is certainly a gloomy prospect and, unlike other chronicles of the contemporary wasteland, this account does not end by prescribing its own particular panacea, political or otherwise. Nor does it propose new institutional arrangements to contain the situation. It merely attempts to describe the position, trace how it has come about and indicate its likely future development. Yet the situation is far from hopeless. Society is changing with unprecedented rapidity in unanticipated directions. People are reacting to the new conditions with new patterns of living and new ideas. While the state desperately strives to maintain control, the situation has long passed the ability of politicians and bureaucrats to predict and manage it. The attempt to do so by rationalizing production and controlling labour through the application of industrial Taylorism to education and training is but one option facing society today. It has loomed large throughout the MSC's narrowly vocational approach to school curricula and its dismantling of traditional training. But there are other possible ways to utilize the opportunities which new technology presents. Rather than to further divide and direct intensified labour into isolated and repetitive tasks, new technology has the potential to lighten and diversify work, breaking down the divisions between separated occupations by increasing communication between them.

As control and all information passes increasingly to an elite, however, the contribution which those relegated to routine part-work could make is ignored. Stripped of our responsibilities and knowledge, we are left uncomprehending of processes as wholes. Society thus misses the unique historical opportunity which new technology presents it with. Because, for new technology to work most effectively requires a sharing of resources among those who operate it and an extension of their creative abilities in new relationships. Machinery so used may be transformed into new tools of human adaptability and resource. Instead of adapting the mass of the people to the machinery, the powers of computing and control systems to handle vast quantities of data with precision and mechanical certitude can be utilized to leave people free to inform the system with their unique qualities of imagination and creativity. For the qualities of computers and people complement one another, so that the best results are not achieved by trying to make people behave like machines.

The paradigm of vocationalism presently dominant in education and training only reinforces the tendency to reduce human intelligence towards the on or off replicative certainty of a machine. But vocational training need not mean such a narrowing of interest and reduction of skill; any more than academic education should represent a divorce from practical ability and direct experience. Real vocational education could become a broadening and deepening of the specific skills of a craft through their practical application in a variety of different situations, as well as through an understanding of the interrelations between the different uses to which they can be put and in which they can be developed. Similarly, genuine study in a science or an art implies practical and not merely theoretical knowledge of all the processes involved. Within such a framework specialization is of course possible, but not merely reduced to the certain completion of individual routine tasks; rather, towards the integration of existing knowledge and technique to produce new creation or discovery, as implied in the old notions of a masterwork or masterpiece as the end product of a period of apprenticeship and improving.

Such a genuinely vocational education could be fostered in schools and colleges by adopting a project-based approach to practical learning tasks. Students would then use their educational institutions and the teachers in them as a resource, the usefulness of which would be judged by the help they provided in the achievement of a goal. Projects that would develop and integrate specific understanding with art and craft skills would have to be recognized as socially necessary and not mere time-filling exercises without other purpose. They could only be evaluated in actual use to society and not against the more or less arbitrary criteria of examinations or the behaviouristic testing of itemized competencies. Where this approach has been adopted, even within the confines of compulsory state schooling and sometimes also with the resources made available by TVEI programmes, it has advanced the abilities and theoretical understanding of the young people involved. They have discovered new knowledge about themselves and the world in new cooperative ways of working. The syllabi of some of the new GCSEs also allow for investigative activities through projects and experimentation. However, within an education system with the primary purpose of allocating labour to unequal positions in an occupational hierarchy posited upon the distinction between mental and manual labour, any successes of an integrative, project-based approach can be no more than isolated indicators of the wasted opportunities of the majority.

Training and control

Vocationalism that represents in reality a new means to control and manipulate new entrants to the labour market only enhances the role of schools in selecting and allocating labour to unequal positions in the workforce. As Paul Willis wrote (xv, 1987), 'The more the school curriculum is vocationalised, the deeper and earlier will class reproduction take root'. Not only are the immediate social effects of this approach harmful, increasing competition between individuals instead of encouraging cooperation between them; the long-term, educational consequences are also disastrous. Imagination is constricted by application to specialized and subdivided tasks. Evaluation is reduced to a behaviouristic determination of competence. The illusion is sustained that all human abilities are measurable and quantifiable. The human facility of integrating apparently unconnected and discrete events into new meaningful wholes is disregarded. Machine intelligence in marshalling and presenting data to order is confused with the human intelligence that alone can interpret that information. Abstract representation of reality is privileged over the unique human imagination of things other than they already are.

This approach to learning and to the world is potentially disastrous since its attachment to predictable routines and repeatable, quantifiable results precludes the imagination of qualitative change. Vocationalism restricts practical experience to the certain completion of itemized competencies unrelated to other associated skills. It cannot comprehend theoretical understanding of systems as wholes. It is thus unable to anticipate and meet change. Yet this vocational approach has evolved just as social change is accelerating and technical change is developing exponentially. In face of this challenge vocationalism encourages only passivity and empiricism. The accreditation of criterion-referenced competencies reduced towards their simplest on/off, binary components endows machines and systems with activity and determination. Control and comprehension rest with the managers and systems analysts who alone establish the programmes for others to operate. They alone think by analogy and in terms of wholes rather than parts. This is in fact the most inefficient and least flexible way of utilizing the new technology. Such systems lack the robustness needed to develop and change, while they are liable to breakdown at all points.

As technology develops, the piece by piece addition of new modules certifying certain competence to complete new operations onto old, previously systematized and accredited skills, cannot lead to the control and understanding of the new processes. For the sum of the parts does not necessarily add up to the whole. In fact it mirrors the mass production of prefabricated units so manufactured that neither care, knowledge nor dexterity are required for their assembly. But the new vocationalism is not designed to give the new workforce the skills and understanding to operate and direct new technology to its most efficient use. It is designed to divest workers of such understanding and control over processes which they have beyond that considered necessary for them by their employers. It is being used to further rationalize, divide and control the workforce instead of controlling the technology for the benefit of society as a whole.

This is most obvious in the concentration of the new vocationalism upon 'work-relevant', 'work-related' and 'work-specific' tasks. As has been seen, consideration of wider social and moral issues has been ruled out of the syllabi of certain vocational courses. There is no longer room for even the gesture towards liberal studies that was once compulsory within day-release apprenticeships at colleges, for instance. While the MSC specifically indicated that political questions were beyond the concerns of the Social and Life Skills component of YTS. The more the new vocational paradigm gains dominance within education, the more real education will take place outside educational institutions. Perhaps it is only here, beyond the limitations of traditional disciplines and the even more constrictive practices of the new vocationalism, that the new conceptions of humanity's changing relations to the world can develop in the course of struggles to change that world. For, as scientific understanding is increasingly restricted to an elite, the ability to make connections between apparently disconnected events and thus creatively discover the reasons for what is happening withers. This process in education coincides with the domination of nearly all sources of information by mass media which daily confuse fact and fiction and reduce complex issues towards simple images. In combination with other tendencies, this is steadily reinforcing the effective disenfranchisement of the majority of the population from public debate and democratic participation in society.

Yet even in this increasingly imaginary and disinformed world, the reality of continued and accelerating economic crisis and its gathering social and ecological consequences impinges insistently upon popular consciousness. It cannot be long before this consciousness is embodied in political forms that will meet with mounting repression and reaction; and/or in populist movements aiding and abetted by that reaction to heighten irrational scapegoating. These developments will increasingly marginalize the state's educational institutions. While the developments that have been outlined in education render schools and colleges less able to act to counter hysteria and irrationality. Their heightened role in selecting and allocating labour will clearly identify them as part of the problem rather than as part of the solution. Real education – the creative development from old knowledge of new ideas to comprehend and deal with the changing situation – can then only develop beyond their walls.

This however, may be a part of a necessary development towards a society in which one day surely education will no longer be synonymous with schooling but will be recognized as a life-long process. The distinction between the educated and the uneducated would then be eroded, along with the division between mental and manual labour. Scientific knowledge about nature and society might then be shared and not divided. Work, learning and enjoyment could be united in creation, so that there would be no longer the disjunction of school from work and no problem of transition between them. At last education would be integral to life and life an education.

Bibliography

Note: For the different situation in Scotland see McPherson, A. & Raab, C. *The Making of Scottish Educational Policy since 1945*, forthcoming from Edinburgh University Press.

Ainley, P. (1987) *What a Performance: Profiling competencies as a measure of skill*, London, London University Institute of Education Post-16 Centre occasional papers (No. 3).

Allen, S. (1974) 'Some Theoretical Problems in the Study of Youth', first published in the *Sociological Review*, London, Vol. 16, No. 3, 1968, and reprinted in Williams, W. 1974.

Annett, J. & Sparrow, J. (1983) 'Transfer of Training, Basic Issues: Policy Implications: How to Promote Transfer. A report for the Manpower Services Commission', Warwick University, unpublished author's draft, December.

Ashton, D. & Field, D. (1976) *Young Workers*. London, Hutchinson.

Atkinson J. (1984) Work at the Institute of Manpower Studies reported in *Executive Post*. London, No. 190, 15/5.

Austen, R. (1984) 'Black Girls in the Youth Training Scheme', unpublished M.Sc. in Race and Ethnic Relations. Birmingham, Aston University.

Banks, O. (1968) *Sociology of Education*. London, Batsford.

Barker-Lunn, J. (1971) *Social Class, Attitudes and Achievement: Two subsidiary studies from the 'Streaming' research data*. Slough, NFER.

Bates, I. (ed) (1974) *Schooling for the Dole? The new vocationalism*. London, Macmillan.

Bazalgette, J. (1978) *School Life and Work Life: A study of transition in the inner city'*. *London, Hutchinson.*

Benn, C. (1980) 'Selection Still Blocks the Growth of Comprehensives'. *Where*. London, No. 158, May, pp. 8–11.

Benn, C. & Simon, B. (1970) *Half Way There: A report on the British comprehensive school reform*. Maidenhead, McGraw-Hill.

Benn, C. & Fairley, J. (eds) (1986) *Challenging the MSC on Jobs, Training and Education*. London, Pluto.

Berg, I. (1971) *Education and Jobs: The great training robbery*. Boston, MA., Beacon Press.

Berger, B. (1963) 'Adolescence and Beyond', *Social Problems*. New York, Vol. 10, Spring, pp. 294–408.

Bernstein, B. (1971, 1974 & 1977) *Class Codes and Control*. 3 vols., London, Routledge.

(1971) 'On the Classification and Framing of Educational Knowledge' in Hopper, E. (ed) *Readings in the Theory of Educational Systems*. London, Hutchinson.

Birmingham Trades Council Union Resource Centre (1984) *The Great Training Robbery*. An interim report on the role of private agencies within the Youth Training Scheme in the Birmingham and Solihull area.

(1987) Report of the Labour Movement Enquiry into Youth Unemployment and Training.

Black, H. (1980) 'The Forms and Functions of Assessment' in Burgess, T. & Adams, E.

Blackwell, T. & Seabrook, J. (1985) *A World Still to Win: The reconstruction of the post-war working class*. London, Faber.

Bloomhead, S. (1987) 'Youth Unemployment and the Growth of the "New Further Education" ' in Coles, B.

Bowles, S. & Gintis, H. (1976) *Schooling in Capitalist America*. New York, Basic Books.

Braverman, H. (1974) '*Labour and Monopoly Capitalism: The degradation of work in the twentieth century*'. New York, Monthly Review Press.

Burgess, T. & Adams, E. (eds) (1980) *Outcomes of Education*, London, Macmillan.

Burke, E. & Lewis, D. (1974–5) 'Standards of Reading: A critical review of some recent studies', *Educational Research*. Abingdon, Vol. 17, No. 3, pp. 163–74.

Carter, M. (1962) *Home, School and Work: A study of the education and employment of young people in Britain*. Oxford, Pergamon.

Central Policy Review Staff (1980) *Education, Training and Industrial Performance*. London, HMSO.

Centre for Contemporary Cultural Studies (1981) *Unpopular Education, Schooling and Social Democracy in England since 1945*. London, Hutchinson.

Channan, G. & Gilchrist, K. (1974) *What School is For*. London, Methuen.

Cherry, N. (1980) 'Ability, Education and Occupational Functioning' in Watts, A., Super, D. & Kidd, J. (eds) *Career Development in Britain*. Cambridge, CRAC and Hobsons.

Clarke, J. & Jefferson, T. (1975) *Working Class Youth Cultures*, Occasional Paper of the Centre for Contemporary Cultural Studies, Birmingham.

Coates, K. & Silburn, R. (1970) *Poverty: The forgotten Englishman*. Harmondsworth Middlesex, Penguin.

Cole, M. & Skelton, B. (eds) (1980) *Blind Alley: Youth in a Crisis of Capitalism*. Ormskirk, Lancs. Hesketh, Introduction.

Coles, B. (ed) (1987) *Young Careers: The search for jobs and the new vocationalism*. Milton Keynes, Open University Press.

Commission for Racial Equality (1984) *Racial Equality and the Youth Training Scheme*. London, CRE.

Cooley, M. (no date) *Architect or Bee? The human/technology relationship*, Hand and Brain. Langley Technical Services, Slough.

Corrigan, P. (1979) *Schooling the Smash Street Kids*. London, Macmillan.

Crosland, A. (1956) *The Future of Socialism*. London, Cape.

Cuming, D. (1983) *School-Leavers, Qualifications and Employment*. 6 Holgate, Nottingham.

Curtis, S. (1952) *Education in Britain since 1900*. Dakers.

Dale, R. (1983) 'You Ain't Seen Nothing Yet: The prospects for education' in Wolpe, A. & Donald, J.

Davies, B. (1986) *Threatening Youth: Towards a national youth policy*. Milton Keynes, Open University Press.

Davies, T. & Mason, C. (1986) *Shutting Out the Inner City Worker: Recruitment and training practices of large employers in central London*. Bristol, SAUS, Bristol University.

Department of Education and Science (1984) *The Youth Training Scheme in Further Education 1983–4: London, An HMI survey*.

(1979) 'Statistics of Education'

(1985) *Report by HMI on the Effects of Local Authority Expenditure*

Policies on Education Provision in England in 1985.
(1986) *Action on Teacher Supply in Maths, Physics and Technology.*
Dittmar, N. (1976) *Sociolinguistics: A critical survey of theory and application*, trans. P. Sand, P. Seuren & K. Whiteley, London, Edward Arnold.
Donald, J. (1979) *Green Paper: Noise of Crisis.* London, Screen Education.
Dore, R. (1976) *The Diploma Disease.* London, Unwin Educational.
Douglas, J., Ross, S. & Simpson, H. (1968) *All Our Future.* London, Peter Davies.
Downes, D. (1966) *The Delinquent Solution.* London, Routledge.
Durkheim, E. (1977) *The Evolution of Educational Thought: Lectures on the formation and development of secondary education in France*, trans. P. Collins. London, Routledge.
Eversley, J. (1986) 'Trade Union Responses to the MSC' in Benn & Fairley.
Ferguson, T. & Cunnison, J. (1952) *The Young Wage Earner.* Oxford, Oxford University Press.
Ferri, E. (1971) *Streaming: Two Years Later.* Slough, NFER.
Finn, D. (1974) 'Leaving School and Growing Up: Work experience in the juvenile labour market' in Bates.
(1982) 'Whose Needs? Schooling and the "needs" of industry' in Rees, T. & Atkinson, P. (eds).
(1984) Untitled draft submission to the National Labour Movement Enquiry into Youth Unemployment and Training, unpublished.
(1987) *Training Without Jobs, New Deals and Broken Promises.* London, Macmillan.
Finn, D. & Markall, G. (1981) *Young People and the Labour Market: A case study.* London, Department of Employment.
Forester, T. (1979) 'Children at Work'. London, *New Society* 1/11.
Freestone, P. (1939) 'The Vocational Interests of Children', *Occupational Psychology.* Leicester, Vol. 13.
Frith, S. (1980) 'Education, Training and the Labour Process' in Cole, M. & Skelton, B.
Further Education and Curriculum Review and Development Unit (1978) London, *Experience, Reflection, Learning: Suggestions for organisers of schemes of UVP.*
(1979) *A Basis for Choice.*
(1980) *Day Release – A desk study.*

(1982) *Competency in Teaching.*

Ginzberg, E. (1971) foreword to Berg, I.

Ginzberg, E., Ginzberg, S., Axelrad, S. & Herma, S. (1951) *Occupational Choice: An approach to a general theory.* Columbia, Columbia University Press.

Goodman, P. (1962) *Compulsory Miseducation.* London, Penguin.

Gorz, A. (1982) *Farewell to the Working Class: An essay on post-industrial socialism,* trans. M. Sonenscher. London, Pluto.

Green, E. (1948) 'Education for Citizenship' in Tracey, H. (ed) *The British Labour Party* Vol. 2, London, Caxton.

Grosch, P. (1987) 'The New Sophists: The work and assumptions of the FEU' in Holt M. Eastbourne, Sussex.

Hall, S. (1983) Introduction to Wolpe & Donald.

Halsey, A. (ed) (1972) *Educational Priority,* Vol. 1, London, HMSO.

(1977) 'The Birth of Educational Priority Areas' in Field, F. (ed) *Education and the Urban Crisis.* London, Routledge.

Halsey, A., Floud, J. & Martin, I. (1965) *Social Class and Educational Opportunity.* London, Heinemann.

Halsey, A., Heath, A. & Ridge, J. (1980) *Origins and Destinations, Family, Class and Education in Modern Britain.* Oxford, OUP.

Hargreaves, D. (1967) *Social Relations in a Secondary School.* London, Routledge.

(1978) *The Two Curricula and the Community.* London, Westminster Studies in Education 1.

(1982) *The Challenge for the Comprehensive School: Culture, curriculum and community.* London, Routledge.

see also ILEA 1984.

Harris, N. (1979) 'Schools and their influence on the delinquent careers of juveniles', *New Era.* Goldsmiths' College, London, 60, No. 1, Jan/Feb.

Harris, R. (1983) 'Access to What? The case for higher education' in Wolpe, A. & Donald, J.

Haystead, J. (1966) 'Social Structure, Awareness Contexts and Processes of Choice', *Sociological Review,* London, Vol. 14.

Herford, M. (1969) 'School to Work' in Caplan, G. & Lebovics, S. (eds) *Adolescence: Psychosocial perspectives.* New York, Basic Books.

HMSO (1943) *Report of the Committee of the Secondary Schools Examination Council, Curriculum and Examinations in Secondary Schools* (The Norwood Report), London.

(1954) *Early Leavers* (Central Advisory Council Report).

(1959) *15 to 18* (the Crowther Report).

(1963a) *Half Our Future* (the Newsom Report).

(1963b) *Higher Education* (the Robbins Report), Appendix 1.

(1965) *Careers Guidance in Schools*, DES Educational Pamphlet No. 48.

(1967) *Children and Their Primary Schools* (the Plowden Report), Appendix 9.

(1972) *Parents' Attitudes to Education* (report by J. Bryunner).

(1974) *Unqualified, Untrained and Unemployed*, Report of a Working Party set up by the National Youth Employment Council.

(1975) *A Language for Life* (the Bullock Report).

(1977) *Education in Schools: A consultative document* (Cmnd 6869).

(1979) *Aspects of Secondary Education in England* (HMI Secondary Report).

(1985a) *Better Schools* (Cmnd 9469).

(1985b) *Education for All*, The Report of the Committee of Inquiry into the Education of Children from Ethnic Minority Groups (the Swann Report).

(1985c) *Vocational Education and Training for Young People*, Report by the Comptroller and Auditor General, Department of Employment and Manpower Services Commission: (Cmnd 497).

(1986) *Working Together – Education and training* (Cmnd 9823).

Hill, J. & Scharff, D. (1976) *Between Two Worlds: Aspects of the transition from school to work*. Richmond, Surrey, Careers Consultants Ltd.

Hinton, M. (1979) *Comprehensive Schools: A Christian's View*. London, SCM Press.

Hirschhorn, L. (1984) *Beyond Mechanisation: Work and technology in a post-industrial age*. Boston, MA., MIT Press.

Hoggart, R. (1958) *The Uses of Literacy*. London, Penguin.

Holly, D. (1977) 'Education and the Social Relations of a Capitalist Society' in Young, M. & Whitty, G.

Holt., J. (1964) *How Children Fail*. London, Pitman.

Holt, M. (1987) *Skills and Vocationalism: The easy answer*. Milton Keynes, Open Univeristy Press.

Howells, D. (1980) 'The Manpower Services Commission: The first five years', *Public Administration*. Oxford, Autumn.

Husen, T. (1972) *Social Background and Educational Career*. Paris, OECD.

ILEA (1975) *Proposals from an Inspectorate working party on improved cooperative educational provision by schools and colleges for low achieving 15 to 19 year olds.*

(1984) *Improving Secondary Schools:* Report of the Committee on the Curriculum and Organisation of Secondary Schools chaired by D. Hargreaves.

(1985) Race, Sex and Class, a policy for equality, 1, 2 & 3.

Illich, D. (1971) *Deschooling Society*, New York, Boyars.

Income Data Services Ltd (1985) *Youth Training Scheme.* London, Study 293, July.

Jackson, B. (1964) *Streaming: An education system in miniature.* London, Routledge.

(1968) *Working Class Community: Some general notions raised by a series of studies in Northern England.* London, Routledge.

(1971) 'The Student's World' in Silberman, M. (ed) *The Experience of Schooling*, New York, Holt Rhinehart.

Jackson, B. & Marsden, D. (1962) *Education and the Working Class: Some general themes raised by a study of 88 working-class children in a northern industrial city.* London, Routledge.

Jahoda, G. (1963) 'School Leavers' Recall of the Interview with the Y.E.O.', *Occupational Psychology.* Leicester, Vol. 37, No. 2, April.

Jenkins, R. (1959) *The Labour Case.* London, Penguin.

Johnson, R. (1983) 'Educational Politics: The old and the new' in Wolpe & Donald

Johnson, S. (1963) 'Life of Milton' in *Samuel Johnson, Poetry and Prose* selected by M. Wilson, London, Hart-Davis.

Keegan, W. (1985) *Britain Without Oil.* London, Penguin.

Keil, E., Riddell, C. & Green, B. (1974) 'Youth and Work, Problems and Perspectives', first published in the *Sociological Review*, London, Vol. 14, No. 2 July 1966 and reprinted in Williams, W.

Kitchen, P. (1944) *From Learning to Earning.* London, Faber.

Kogan, M. (1975) *Educational Policy Making.* London, Allen and Unwin.

Labour, Party (1981) *16–19: Learning for Life, a discussion document.*

(1985) Charter for Youth.

(1986) 'Education and Training: Options for Labour', $1 from Barry Sheerman MP at the House of Commons.

(1987) *New Skills for Britain: Labour's Programme for National Renewal.*

Labour Party/TUC (1984) *A Plan for Training*. London.

Lacey, C. (1970) *Hightown Grammar*. Manchester, Manchester University Press.

Lambert, A. (1976) 'The Sisterhood' in Hammersley, M. & Woods, P. *The Process of Schooling*. London, Routledge.

Lawrence, D. (1956) *Twilight in Italy*. London, Heinemann.

Leavis, F. & Thompson, D. (1942) *Culture and Environment: The training of critical awareness*. London, Chatto.

Levitas, M. (1974) *Marxist Perspectives in the Sociology of Education*. London, Routledge.

Lewis, M. (1955) *The Importance of Illiteracy*. London, Harrap.

Lindley, R. (1980) *Economic Change and Employment Policy*. London, Macmillan.

Lindsay, K. (1969) *School and Community*. Oxford, Pergamon.

Liversidge, W. (1962) 'Life Chances' first published in the *Sociological Review*, London, Vol. 10, No. 1, and reprinted in Williams, W. 1974.

London County Council (1961) *London Comprehensive Schools: A survey of sixteen schools*. London.

Loney, M. (1983) 'The YOP, Requiem or, Rebirth?' in Fiddy, R. (ed) *In Place of Work: Policy and provision for the young unemployed*. Brighton, Falmer.

MacLennan, E., Fitz, J. & Sullivan, J. (1985) *Working Children*. Low Pay Unit, London.

Manpower Services Commission (1977) *Analytic Techniques for Skill Comparison*, Vols I and II. Sheffield.

(1982) 'Youth Task Group Report'. Sheffield.

(1983) 'A New Training Initiative, A Consultative Document'. Sheffield.

(1984a) 'Corporate Plan 1984–88'. Sheffield.

(1984b) *Ethnic Minorities and the Youth Training Scheme*. Sheffield.

(1984c) *Instructional Guide to Social and Life Skills*. Sheffield.

(1985) *'Development of the Youth Training Scheme'*. Sheffield.

Markall, G. (1982) 'The Job Creation Programme: Some Reflections on its Passing' in Rees, T. & Atkinson, P.

Marks, J. & Pomian-Srzednicki, M. (1985) *Standards in English Schools*, Second Report. London, National Council for Educational Standards.

Marland, M. (1980) *Education for the Inner City*. London, Heinemann.

Marsden, D. (1969) 'Which Comprehensive Principle?' *Comprehen-*

sive Education. London, No. 13, Autumn.

Martell, G. 'The Politics of Reading and Writing' in Dale, R., Esland, G. & Macdonald, M. *Schooling and Capitalism: A sociological reader*. London and Milton Keynes, Routledge and Open University, 1976.

Marwick, A. (1980) *Class, Image and Reality in Britain and the USA since 1930*. London, Collins.

Marx, K. (1889) *Capital* Vol. 1 (fascimile edition London, George Allen and Unwin 1971).

(1966) *'Der Politische Indifferentismus', Werke*, Vol. 33, Berlin, Dietz Verlag Berlin, pp. 299–300.

Matthews, G. (1963) 'Post-School Adaptation of Educationally Sub-Normal Boys', unpublished M.Ed. Thesis. Manchester, University of Manchester.

Mays, J. (1962) *Education and the Urban Child*. Liverpool, Liverpool University Press.

Mead, M. (1944) *Coming of Age in Samoa*. London, Pelican.

Meighan, R. (1981) *A Sociology of Educating*. New York, Holt-Rinehart.

Midwinter, E. (1972) *Social Environment and the Urban School*. London, Ward Lock.

(1973) *Patterns of Community Education*. London, Ward Lock.

Miller, D. & Form, W. (1964) *Industrial Sociology*. London, Harper.

Moon, J. (1983) 'Policy change in direct government responses to UK unemployment', *Journal of Public Policy*. Cambridge, No. 3, part 3.

Moon, J. & Richardson, J. (1985) *Unemployment in the UK: Politics and policies*. London, Gower.

Moor, C. (1976) *From School to Work: Effective counselling and guidance*, SAGE Studies in Social and Educational Change, Vol.3, London, SAGE.

Moore, R. (1985) *Education, Training and Production: A critique of the current debate*. London, Faculty of EHSS Research Report, Polytechnic of the South Bank.

Moser, C. & Hall, J. (1954) 'Social Grading of Occupations' in Glass, D. (ed) *Social Mobility in Britain*. London, Routledge.

Murdock, G. & Phelps, G. (1973) *Mass Media and the Secondary School*. London, Macmillan.

Murray, N. (1986) 'The Press and Ideology in Thatcher's Britain', *Race and Class* XXVII, 3. London.

Musgrave, P. (1967) 'Towards a Sociological Theory of Occupational Choice', *Sociological Review*, London, Vol. 15.

Nash, R. (1973) *Classrooms Observed*. London, Routledge.

National Association for the Care and Resettlement of Offenders (1987) 'Facing the Problem', Press Release 22/6. London.

Newson, J. & E. (1963) *Patterns of Infant Care in an Urban Community*. London, Penguin.

Parker, S. (1977) 'Industry and Education' in Brown, R., Child, J., Parker, S. & Smith, M. (eds) *The Sociology of Industry*. London, Allen & Unwin.

Peck, J., Lloyd, P. & Carter, D. (1936) *The Impact of New Funding Regimes on YTS: The experience of ex-Mode B1 providers*. Manchester, North West Industrial Research Unit, University of Manchester.

Polanyi, M. (1962) 'Tacit Knowing: Its bearing on some problems of philosophy', *Reviews of Modern Physics*. New York, Vol. 34, No. 4, October.

Pollert, A. (1986) 'The MSC and Ethnic Minorities' in Benn & Fairley 1986.

Pye, D. (1968) *The Nature and Art of Workmanship*, Cambridge, Cambridge University Press.

Raffe, D. (1986a) *The Context of the YTS: An analysis of its strategy and development*, CES working paper No. 86/11, Edinburgh, University of Edinburgh.

(1986b) 'Unemployment and School Motivation: the case of truancy', *Educational Research*. Edinburgh, Vol. 38, No. 1.

Reay, D. (1980) *Hidden Streaming in the Classroom*. TSW Education, Leicester, Forum, Spring.

Reeder, D. (1979) 'A Recurring Debate: Education and industry' in Bernbaum (ed) *Schooling in Decline*. London, Macmillan.

Rees, T. & Atkinson, P. (eds) (1982) *Youth Unemployment and State Intervention*, Introduction. London, Routledge.

Reynolds, D. & Sullivan, M. (1987) *The Comprehensive Experiment*. Brighton, Falmer.

Roberts, K. (1968) 'The Entry into Employment: An approach towards a general theory', *Sociological Review*, London, Vol. 16.

(1971) *From school to work, a study of the Youth Employment Service*, Netwon Abbot, David & Charles.

Robertson, J. (1985) *Future Work: Jobs, Self-employment and Leisure after the Industrial Age*. Aldershot, Hants, Temple Smith.

Rogers, R. (1980) *Crowther to Warnock: How fourteen reports tried to change children's lives*. London, Heinemann.

Rosenbrock, H. (1977) 'The Future of Control', *Automatica*, Oxford, Pergamon, Vol. 13.

Rosenthal, R. & Jacobsen, L. (1968) *Pygmalion in the Classroom*. New York, Holt Rinehart.

Rubinstein, D. (1969) *School Attendance in London 1870–1904: A social history*. Hull, Hull University.

Rubinstein, D. & Simon, B. (1973) *The Evolution of the Comprehensive School*, 1926–71. London, Routledge.

Rutter, M., Maughan, B., Mortimore, P. & Ouston, J. (1979) *Fifteen Thousand Hours: Secondary schools and their effects on children*. Wells, Somerset, Open Books.

Ryrie, A. & Weir, D. (1977) *Serving Their Time*. Edinburgh, Scottish Council for Research in Education.

Sako, M. & Dore, R. (1986) 'How the YTS Helps Employers', *The Employment Gazette*. London, June.

Sarup, M. (1978) *Marxism and Education*. London, Routledge.

(1982) *Education, State and Crisis: A Marxist perspective*. London, Routledge.

(1986) *The Politics of Multiracial Education*. London, Routledge.

Scofield, P., Preston, E. & Jacques, E. (1983) *The Tories' Poisoned Apple*. Leeds, Independent Labour Publications.

Searle, C. (1975) *Classrooms of Resistance*. London, Writers' and Readers' Publishing Cooperative.

Selbourne, D. (1981) *Against Socialist Illusion: A radical argument*. London, Macmillan.

Sharpe, R. (1975) *Education and Social Control: A study in progressive primary education*. London, Routledge.

Sheldrake, J. & Vickerstaff, S. (1987) *The History of Industrial Training in Britain*. Godstone, Surrey, Avebury.

Sherman, B. (1986) *Working at Leisure*. London, Methuen.

Showler, B. & Sinfield, A. (eds) (1980) *The Workless State, Studies in Unemployment*. Blackwells, Oxford, Martin Robertson.

Sinfield, A. (1981) *What Unemployment Means*, Blackwells, Oxford, Martin Robertson.

Smith, R. (ed) (1975) *Regaining Educational Leadership*, Chichester, Sussex. John Wiley.

Start, K. & Wells, B. (1972) *The Trend of Reading Standards*. Slough, NFER.

Stedman, J. (1980) *Progress in Secondary Schools, Findings from the National Child Development Study*. London, National

Children's Bureau.

Swann, B. & Turnbull, M. (1978) *Records of Interest to Social Scientists 1919–39: Employment and unemployment.* London, HMSO.

Tawney, R. (1931) *Equality*. London, Unwin Books.

Tower Hamlets Trades Council (1981) *Opportunity Knocks: A discussion paper for Trades Unionists.* London.

Townsend, P. & Abel-Smith, B. (1965) *The Poor and the Poorest.* Occasional Paper on Social Administration. London, No. 17.

Training Services Agency (1975) *Vocational Preparation for Young People: A discussion document.* Sheffield.

(1976) 'Five Year Flow-Review'.

(1977) *Young People and Work* (The Holland Report). Sheffield.

(1981) *A New Training Initiative: An agenda for action.* Sheffield.

Turner, R. (1964) *The Social Context of Ambition.* Novato, California, Chandler.

Venables, E. (1968) *Leaving School and Starting Work.* Oxford, Pergamon.

Vernon, B. (1982) *Ellen Wilkinson 1891–1947.* Bekenham, Kent, Croom Helm.

Waugh, C. (1982) 'Really Useful Knowledge', *Schooling and Culture.* London, Issue 12.

Webb, J. (1962) 'The Sociology of a School', *British Journal of Sociology*. London, Routledge, Vol. 13.

Webster, J. (1982) *Reading Matters, A Practical Philosophy.* London, McGraw Hill.

West Midlands County Council (1986) *A Different Reality: Report of the review panel* from County Hall, Birmingham.

Whitney, O. (1961) *A Majority without Education*, Southern District WEA, Southampton.

Whitty, G. (1983). *Missing: a policy on the curriculum* in Wolpe, A. & Donald, J.

Williams, S. (1981) *Politics Is for People.* London, Penguin.

(1985) *A Job to Live: The impact of tomorrow's technology on work and society*. London, Penguin.

Williams W. (ed) (1974) *Occupational Choice.* London, Allen and Unwin.

Willis, P. (1977) *Learning to Labour: How working class kids get working class jobs*, Aldershot, Hants, Saxon House.

(1985) *The Social Conditions of Young People in Wolverhampton.* Wolverhampton, Wolverhampton Borough Council.

(1987) Foreword to Finn.
Wilmott, A. & Nuttall, D. (1975) *The Reliability of Examinations at 16 Plus*. London, Schools Council/Methuen.
Wilmott, P. (1966) *Adolescent Boys in East London*. London, Routledge.
Wolpe, A. & Donald, J. (eds) (1983) *Is There Anyone There From Education? Education after Thatcher*. London, Pluto.
Woodward, J. (1965) *Industrial Organisation: Theory and practice*, Oxford, Oxford University Press.
Young, D. (1967) 'Comprehensive Schools: The danger of a counter-revolution', *Comprehensive Education*. London, No. 5.
Young, M. (ed) (1971) '*Knowledge and Control: New directions in the sociology of education*'. London, Macmillan.
Young, M. & Whitty, G. (1977) *Society, State and Schooling*, Brighton, Falmer.
Youthaid (1984) *What Opportunities for Youth?* London.
(1985) *The Youth Training Scheme, Youthaid's evidence to the House of Commons Employment Committee.*

Index